TRUE LEADERSHIP

TRUE LEADERSHIP

SECOND EDITION

Habiger Institute *for* Catholic Leadership

≈

Preface by Michael J. Naughton

Introduction by Jonathan Reyes

CLUNY
Providence, Rhode Island

CLUNY MEDIA SECOND EDITION, 2021

For more information regarding this title
or any other Cluny Media publication,
please write to info@clunymedia.com, or to
Cluny Media, P.O. Box 1664, Providence, RI 02901

VISIT US ONLINE AT WWW.CLUNYMEDIA.COM

For information regarding The Habiger Institute for Catholic Leadership,
please visit www.stthomas.edu/habiger/ or call 651-962-5700.

For bulk orders, please email info@clunymedia.com
or write to Cluny Media, P.O. Box 1664, Providence, RI 02901.

ISBN: 978-1952826665

Cover design by Clarke & Clarke
Cover image: *Christ the Saviour* (*Pantokrator*), encaustic,
6th century, Saint Catherine's Monastery, Mount Sinai
Courtesy of Wikimedia Commons

CONTENTS

PART III

THE NATURE AND PURPOSE OF INSTITUTIONS

〜〜

PREFACE

SINCE OUR ESTABLISHMENT in 1993, Catholic Studies in the College of Arts and Sciences at the University of St. Thomas (Minnesota) educates and forms leaders for the Church and the World who follow Christ and exercise their gifts to contribute to the common good. In 2006, we created the Habiger Institute for Catholic Leadership within our Center for Catholic Studies as a key instrument in accomplishing that mission. The Institute answers the call to provide students a unique context for leadership formation that goes beyond the development of skills to a more organic and collaborative model of Catholic leadership, one firmly rooted in Christian faith and character.

At the heart of the Habiger Institute's work is the Leadership Intern program. This program identifies promising students who have demonstrated leadership capacity and offers them a dynamic opportunity to develop their leadership potential and mature in fortitude. The program has many facets: vision retreats, service to the campus and to the wider community, dialogue with invited speakers, and a one week immersion Spring Institute. The Spring Institute is a capstone integrating the themes of this book with unique experiences and conversations with leaders in the areas of business, education, politics, law and social services. At the core of Leadership Interns program is a weekly meeting at which the Interns receive formation in the principles of Catholic leadership from this book. Hundreds of St. Thomas Catholic Studies students have taken advantage of the program over the years and are now taking on positions of responsibility in family, the professions, society, and the Church.

True Leadership lays out the vision and the principles of leadership formation as they have been developed by the Habiger Institute. Msgr. James Habiger, who endowed the Institute, was fond of quoting Proverbs: *without a vision the people perish.* The Catholic vision of leadership found in this volume draws upon the Church's rich intellectual, social and spiritual tradition. Such a tradition gives deep roots to leaders in a Catholic way of life and in particular a vision of the human person—who has been created out of love, destined for God's Kingdom, and called to participate with Christ in an adventure of building that Kingdom by exercising influence in the world.

It should not surprise us that we should look to the Church's long tradition on the principles of leadership. The Catholic Church has been at the work of building and renewing institutions for over two thousand years. She is the great builder of institutions, of monasteries, religious orders, fraternal organizations, elementary and secondary schools, universities, charities, health care, parishes, dioceses. And while her achievements have also been marked by poor leaders throughout history, the Church has had a remarkable ability to constantly renew, through great leaders, the institutions she has created.

One of the key themes of this book is that leadership takes place within institutions, and to understand leadership is to understand the nature of institutions and how we can renew and strengthen the good they were created to do. And yet we find ourselves in a crisis of institutions. We have increasingly thinned them out morally and spiritually, reducing institutions from a vibrant set of integrated goods to one instrumental or emotive good. So, while many of our institutions have grown in size, they have shrunk in purpose. They have become small spaces both morally and spiritually.

This concern for our institutions and their leadership is being expressed by various scholars and practitioners both religious and secular. Dee Hock, founder and former CEO of Visa, wrote that concealed beneath our physical viruses ravaging our physical well-being is "a global epidemic of institutional failure much greater, and more difficult to recognize and cure." He pinpoints this institutional failure in terms of leaders "unable to achieve the purpose for which they were created."

The differentiating contribution of *True Leadership* is the deep moral and spiritual roots necessary to overcome the crisis of leadership of institutions. Despite all that is written about leadership today, there is a nagging sense of rootlessness in much leadership talk. Slogans and fads and easy techniques are constantly on offer. But given the world that is emerging around us, especially in light of the increasing social unrest of our times, we are in need of a deeper root system that offers a greater coherence to the relationship of leadership and institutional life.

In many respects, the need for roots has been an ongoing theme throughout history. In 1943, the French Jewish philosopher and political activist, Simone Weil, was asked by the French Resistance to prepare a text on the possibilities for rebuilding French society and for effecting a cultural regeneration once the Nazis had been defeated. The essay she wrote was eventually given the title *The Need for Roots*. Weil explained that having roots was "perhaps the most important and least recognized need of the human soul." She was particularly concerned of the West becoming dominated by pragmatism, an agnosticism to the transcendent, a fixation on technical science, and specialization resulting in fragmentation, all of which leaves us morally and spiritually rootless.

Our hope is that *True Leadership* will contribute to the immensely important task of forming Catholic leaders and giving them the necessary roots they will need to weather the grave challenges that confront them, as well as the wisdom to strengthen the institutions they have inherited.

MICHAEL J. NAUGHTON
Koch Chair in Catholic Studies
Director, Center for Catholic Studies
College of Arts and Sciences,
University of St. Thomas, Minnesota

INTRODUCTION

THE HEALTH OF a society is directly dependent on the quality of its leaders. This is simply true. The inverse is also true. Where you find a society in disarray and suffering from a lack of unity and direction, where the people are not thriving and lack a sense of a common good, where institutions languish and reasonable disagreement becomes impossible, where people are driven by fear rather than hope, , there you will also find a lack of good leadership. I suspect that this at least partly explains the massive quantity of leadership books and programs, as well as the ubiquitous rhetoric about leadership, that abound in our educational institutions, businesses, and political discourse. Where people sense that something is wrong with society—as polls keep telling us that they do—one would expect to find a fair amount of concern about forming good leaders.

But the presence of a large number of publications does not necessarily translate into clarity. In fact it can lead to just the opposite. What really is good leadership? What makes someone a good leader?

One challenge we face in trying to answer this question is the prevalent assumption that our social problems can be solved by technical means—political, technological, economic, or sociological. This assumption explains the numerous leadership books that treat leadership as a set of techniques to be mastered—as though the qualities that make an effective leader are reducible to a set of skills and a general desire to do good things and to "be successful," however success is defined. Our age also loves to measure—a good thing in the hard sciences, but a more limited good when it comes to human relationships, which is the space wherein leadership is exercised. Thus there is a temptation to judge a leader simply by the "bottom line," or by some other metric that associates easily measurable outcomes with human success.

There is a truth here: good leaders get things done. But it is insufficient in determining what comprises good leadership.

This is why the book you have in your hands is so important. In this book we have a theological, philosophical, and very practical account of leadership; one that approaches the question holistically. A leader is more than a skilled director. Good leadership is measured by more than stock price or by the number of people served. And it certainly cannot be assessed the number of re-tweets or views of a social media presentation. Influencers may indeed influence, but they are not necessarily leading. To lead is to have a lasting impact on the world, it is to invite others to choose a fundamental direction in life and help them stay the course no matter the challenges. Rhetorical skill, organizational excellence or financial genius alone cannot do this, nor any other technical skills one may acquire. At its core, true leadership is a way of being.

It involves the whole person, from speaking skills and intellectual formation, to character and fundamental commitments. This is a vision of integral Christian leadership. And it takes as its model of leadership Jesus Christ.

Consider how different the model of Christ's leadership is from many ways of leading popularized in our culture. Viewed from the perspective of measurable success, Our Lord's own leadership looked like a failure— at least until the Resurrection. The movement he sought to establish and the institution he was building were seemingly in disarray at the end of his life. His followers, few in number, had been scattered; some had even betrayed and denied him. His was a record of what appeared to be dashed hopes, as can be seen in the pathos-filled words of the disciple on the road to Emmaus: "Jesus of Nazareth, a prophet mighty in deed and word" but whom "our chief priests and rulers delivered up to be condemned to death and crucified . . . *But we had hoped that he was the one to redeem Israel*" (cf. Lk 24:15–21). Of course, the long history since Our Lord's Resurrection tells a very different story. The movement he founded and the institution he established has outlived every empire and nation and spread to the whole world. There is an important lesson in this: To lead like Christ may not fit the world's expectations, but it is the way that the truly lasting things, those that serve the good of the whole human race, are established and grow. It is the only true way of effective leadership.

We might then ask: how did Christ lead? This book is an extended answer to that question, but let us make two observations here. First, Jesus invested in only a few disciples, teaching them how to live and to think—in short how to imitate him. Second, he left an institution to carry his vision from one generation to the next.

To this day, people follow *him*. And if we are to lead as he leads, we must become like him. We must take on Our Lord's mind and heart. We must be conformed to him in our intellect, will and passions. Once we understand this, once we make the decision to pursue him with our minds and wills, then our skills, techniques, and gifts can be put at the service of true leadership for the sake of the world. There are many who lead in the modern world—who get others to follow them or to do certain things— but who are leading in the wrong direction. Genuine leadership has a trajectory and a goal—the good. We have too many examples, culturally, politically and intellectually, of leadership going in the opposite direction. We must decide not merely to lead, but to lead in a certain way in a certain direction: not according to our own desires, but according the model of Christ himself. Only then can we truly be of service to our families, our communities, and our world.

He also established the Church. There is a temptation in this world of social media and its attendant celebrities, be they actors, politicians, financiers or athletes or some combination of all of the above, to reduce leadership to its charismatic form. The great leader, in such a paradigm, is the dynamic individual whose words are re-tweeted and whose face is frequently visible on our screens. He or she writes best-selling books and speaks to large crowds, live or virtual, whether to sell ideas or products. There is real influence here, but it rarely outlasts the life of the leader. How many such voices have come and gone and been forgotten. Even great books, though read again and again cannot interpret themselves and so may be read amiss. Lasting influence, the legacy of true leadership, is always exercised in the context of an institution because institutions preserve a vision, hand on a tradition, and shape events for more than a lifetime. Thus the most effective leadership always involves founding, preserving or reforming institutions for the sake of later generations. In our age, when so many of our institutions are no longer trusted—the press, big business, the government, even the Church—we need to remember this important truth. Great leaders today will need to be more than well-known, they will need to be founders and reformers of institutions—fathers and mothers, bishops and priests, business leaders, elected officials, professors and administrators, executives of NGOs.

Christ's model of leadership, so personal and yet institutional, presents both an invitation and a challenge.

The invitation comes because the vision of leadership presented here requires a commitment. To lead like Christ means accepting his invitation, the one he gave to the rich young man, to set aside our personal attachments and preferences—all of them—and to follow him. This cannot be forced; it can only be offered. We are free to choose to lead like Christ, or to walk away from him. The one thing we cannot do is to the change the choice or pretend it does not exist. Every human hears these words of invitation from Our Lord. It is the central drama of every human life.

This invitation is therefore also a challenge. The promise of an easy life is not one of the promises of God. To choose to lead according to his lights is to choose to stand with Paul and with Peter, and with Saint Mother Teresa and Pope Saint John Paul II; it is to choose to lay everything down for the sake of others in obedience to God the Father. "Not my will, but thy will be done." And the choice comes with a cost.

But it also comes with joy. To say "yes" to this invitation is to say yes to the path of greatest happiness. It is also the path to the greatest good for the world. Consider the influence of just one life on the fortunes of the world, a life completely committed to Christ, leading as he led. Consider the hundreds of thousands of the poorest of the poor who waited for hours simply to walk by Mother Teresa's body. Consider the hundreds of thousands whose lives have been redirected away from self-centeredness to the service of others because of her example. Think of the millions who were liberated from oppressive political regimes by the influence of John Paul on the political events of his day; or the way his slow death, viewed over months on national television, changed the conversation about human dignity, age, and the end of life.

Over the years I have had the privilege of meeting many young men and women who have said yes to Christ's invitation to follow, to sacrifice, and to lead. They, and many others like them, have not chosen an easy life, but they have chosen a great one.

The large number of young people currently making this choice is remarkable, given the obstacles in the way of following Christ's model of leadership. From my own experience there are four common and powerful such obstacles. First, it is easy to be *cynical* about leadership in our age, an age when leaders are frequently known more for their failures and hypocrisy than for their impressive service. Second, it is easy to be *afraid* of taking on leadership roles, especially given the scrutiny leaders are subjected to in the public eye, a scrutiny that wants to highlight scandal and hypocrisy as more newsworthy than faithfulness and commitment. Third, leadership is a *burden*, one that may not be welcome to many. It is easy enough to say: "Why do I have to step forward? Why shouldn't I simply take care of my own life and leave others to themselves? What have I to do with the wider world, or my wider community, or even my neighbor except in so far as they are part of my own success story?" The fourth and perhaps greatest obstacle to responding to Christ's invitation to leadership is: *lack of hope*. It is easy to experience hopelessness in the face of the size and apparent intractability of many modern problems—injustice, corruption, political instability, poverty, racism, and cultural decay. There is also a common personal hopelessness, a pervasive conviction that one cannot succeed in having a meaningful or joy-filled life.

This is a book for those who, despite these temptations, have said "yes" to Christ. It lays out a clear definition of leadership. It affords the opportunity to assess oneself, honestly but positively, in the exercise of leadership. It offers a practical way forward—a road map—for growing into the kind of leader that can truly transform the world for Christ. If you take the time to read and think through this book, and if you choose to make its vision your vision, you will set out on a course that will help you to become the kind of person the world needs. That is the invitation and the promise of this short but powerful book.

Thank you for saying "yes" to Christ's call, and be assured that the Lord will make that "yes" a gift for you and for the world that he loves and gave his life to save.

JONATHAN REYES
Senior Vice President for
Evangelization and Faith Formation
Knights of Columbus

PART I

Understanding True Leadership

CHAPTER 1

WHY A BOOK ON TRUE LEADERSHIP?

AFTER ALL, THERE are dozens, hundreds of books on leadership. The bookstores are crammed full of them. And many of them have good and important things to say. Who would want to add another drop to that Niagara? Why not just find and use some good material already developed? The reason is this: in trying to understand what makes the true leader, we have come across many good partial treatments and many helpful suggestions, but we have not found the kind of integrated understanding of leadership founded on clear principles that we were seeking. This book is an attempt to set down that integrated vision. It is intended explicitly for Christians and for Catholics, since the principles upon which this vision is founded are Christian and Catholic ones. But it may also be of use to any who are concerned about the formation of the next generation of leaders.[1]

---

1. For those looking for valuable leadership insights, especially from a Christian perspective, there are some excellent resources available. From the perspective of management, see Helen Alford and Michael Naughton, *Managing as if Faith Mattered* (University of Notre Dame, 2001). On organizational culture see the work of Patrick Lencioni, *The Advantage* (Jossy-Bass, 2012), and Fr. Robert Spitzer, *The Spirit of Leadership: Optimizing Creativity and Change in Organizations* (Executive Excellence Publishers, June 2000). For a fine consideration of the role of the virtues in leadership see Alexandre Havard, *Virtuous Leadership* (Scepter, 2007). For leadership in business see *The Vocation of the Business Leader* and *Respect in Action* published by the Pontifical Council for Justice and Peace.

GOD'S LEADERSHIP PRINCIPLE

To start at the beginning, we can ask a very basic question: Why should we be concerned about leaders in the first place? Of course we want those who bear responsibility to be good at what they do lest their lack of attention or skill causes us problems. Let those who fly airplanes fly them well; let those who run financial accounts understand their business; let those who cut us open on the operating table know how to close us up again. But this is not precisely leadership; it is rather basic human competence. To speak of leadership is to assume a situation in which there are not only leaders but also followers; not only those in charge, but also those in their charge; not only people who bear responsibility, but also people who depend upon them. It is to presume that we need the help and guidance of others to make our way through life.

It is here that objections begin to arise. After all, are we not independent beings, each possessed of a mind, an ability to judge right from wrong, each with a sense of what we like and don't like, each having a scope for action? Children need guides; but as adults, surely we are capable of determining our own way apart from the actions of others. Why is leadership important? Who really needs leaders, except perhaps the dull or the weak or the lazy?

There are many answers to this fundamental question, answers that will emerge in the course of this book. But the primary reason for our concern for leadership goes to the heart of who we are. It is based on the fact that we were created by another. It can be expressed by this existential truth: everyone is by necessity following someone else. It is what the philosophers mean when they say that we are contingent beings. It is what Jesus means when he so constantly uses the analogy of sheep and shepherds. For him the whole of the human race are so many sheep who need a shepherd lest they end in disaster. In using this image Jesus is not insulting us, treating us like children or denigrating our intelligence. On the contrary he has a very high view of our capabilities and he issues a dauntingly high call toward their attainment. Rather, he is pointing to a basic truth about what it means to be human. We are creatures "on the way," not yet fully created, not yet arrived at our final home, and we do not have within ourselves the capacity to gain that fulfillment by ourselves: not the smartest of us, not the most creative, not the most determined and hard-working. Though we often live under the illusion of such independence, we do not have the capability of "going our own way," of constructing a life for ourselves independent of another's guidance. We were never meant to do this. We are not God; we are created beings, and that means that we are following someone, being told by someone else who we are and what road we need to take to arrive at fulfillment.

At its most profound, this truth is expressed in what has been called since the beginning of the Judeo-Christian tradition the doctrine of the Two Ways. There is a road, a path, a way that leads to life. There is another that leads to death and we must choose which way we will follow. There is an analogy at work here: walking the road that leads to life is not about geography. This way involves an inner journey toward human fulfillment. Not only are we not yet home spatially; beyond that, we are not yet fully created, not yet home in our being. We are followers because we are yearning to become fully created, fully human. Every person walks upon one or the other of these two roads, and ends at one of only two destinations. "I have set before you life and death," said God through Moses to the Israelites, "blessing and curse. Therefore choose life, that you and your descendants may live" (Deut 30:19). The same truth is repeated in the opening psalm that sets the pattern for the whole of that book of inspired prayers: "Blessed is the man who walks not in the counsel of the wicked, but whose delight is the law of the Lord.... For the Lord knows the way of the righteous, but the way of the wicked will perish" (Ps 1:1, 6). Jesus regularly calls his hearers to "follow" him. He points to the two ways, the one, difficult and narrow that leads to life, and the other, broad and easy, that leads to destruction (Mt 7:13). St. Paul in his letter to the Romans distinguishes between those who are servants of God and those who are servants of sin, two categories that between them cover the whole human race (Rom 6:16). Such is the way of things, in the midst of genuine human freedom and admitted human complexity: either we follow God and come at last to our true home, or we turn aside from him and follow another to our ruin. This following of another takes many forms, and those who are dancing the steps along that ruinous path may not always know the ultimate piper of the tune. But known or unknown to us, we are walking a road behind another. There is no truth to the popular myth of self-generated human independence.

God's principle of leadership is evident in the way we are brought into the world. We could have been created fully formed, independent, and ready to act on our own, dropping on our feet from trees or floating down one by one from the sky. Instead, God arranged matters such that the origin of our earthly existence comes through the cooperation of two others, and we begin that existence utterly dependent on those others, not only for our material sustenance but for teaching us our basic humanity: for giving us language and helping us to the mastery of our bodies and our minds. Without leaders, none of us could ever have arrived at adulthood, as a simple material fact. No six-month-old, however full of self-importance and the independent spirit, can stand up and sing "I did it my way." No six-month-old can even stand up.

What is true of us materially in our childhood is true in a different way throughout life, and can be stated by this general principle: the human race makes its way in the world under the exercise of leadership. Whether in family, or in faith, or in politics, or in work and business, or in education, or in the arts and trades, we learn from others, we follow the lead of others, and we in our turn take positions of leadership and influence others. An important corollary to this general principle emerges, which is unavoidable as based on a truth of our nature: the health and strength and wisdom of leaders will determine the health and happiness of the whole people.

GOD'S CONCERN FOR GOOD LEADERS

The great importance of leadership explains the anger of God expressed
so cogently in passages from the Hebrew prophets against leaders, shepherds, who were feeding upon their sheep rather than providing for them.
"'Woe to the shepherds who destroy and scatter the sheep of my pasture!'
says the Lord. 'You have scattered my flock, and have driven them away,
and you have not attended to them. Behold, I will attend to you for your
evil doings, says the Lord'" (Jer 26:1–2). "Woe to my worthless shepherd, who deserts the flock! May the sword smite his arm and his right
eye! Let his arm be wholly withered, his right eye utterly blinded!" (Zec
11:17). It explains the heated indignation of Jesus toward the Pharisees,
blind guides who were leading others astray: "Woe to you, scribes and
Pharisees, hypocrites! because you shut the kingdom of heaven against
men; for you neither enter yourselves, nor allow those who would enter to
go in" (Mt 23:13). It can be seen in the attitude of Paul toward those who
were leading the Galatians away from the truth: "As we have said before,
so now I say again, If any one is preaching to you a gospel contrary to
that which you received, let him be accursed!" (Gal 1:9). It explains why
the Church has always been sterner toward the heretic, the false leader,
than toward the private sinner. It explains our natural anger when we
see destructive results that come from bad leadership or evil influence.
Understandably, we wonder, why didn't those responsible do something
about this? It also explains why, in his very brief life among us, and even
briefer period of public ministry, the divine Son of God spent most of
his time and energy training a small band of leaders. Jesus preached to
crowds, he healed multitudes, and he taught from town to town, but most
carefully he gathered to himself and spent his intimate hours upon a very
few, preparing them to lead. Behind these expressions of God's concern
for leadership one finds this important truth: the leader of the human race
is God himself. He is the Father, the "chief shepherd," the One whom we
need to follow if we are to find our true fulfillment and become who we

are meant to be. God's leadership of the human race finds its incarnation in Christ: "The God of our fathers raised Jesus whom you killed by hanging him on a tree. God exalted him at his right hand as Leader and Savior, to give repentance to Israel and forgiveness of sins" (Acts 5:30–31). The call of obedience to God is a call to follow the proper leader. It is not a call to a merely arbitrary submission to a stronger will, which would be nothing but tyrannical slavery, but instead a summons to a willing obedience to the One who is the source of all life, who made us and who leads us to ourselves. "Lose your life and you will find it" is a paradoxical principle running through all the teaching of Jesus.

There is a further important truth concerning God's leadership principle. While all authority ultimately comes from God the Father, who leads the human race through Christ the Divine Son, God has greatly dignified humanity by giving us a share in his leadership, so that we might bear the joy and responsibility of aiding one another to our final goal. This participation is an aspect of what it means to be created in the image and likeness of God. We are God's children, and he has given us the gift of the Holy Spirit, a share in his Divine nature. He then bestows a measure of his authority upon each of those he calls his children. We share in the kingly office of Jesus: the pope and bishops and priests; parents; those in civil government; teachers; employers and leaders in business; in various ways each one of us. The idea that "everyone is a leader" can seem no more than a trite phrase, a way of artificially making everyone feel good, and if misunderstood can empty the idea of leadership of all serious content. If everyone leads, so it may seem, then effectively no one does. But understood rightly, this idea expresses a profound truth about what it means to be fully human. Not all lead in the same way or with the same degree of responsibility and influence. But all are called, as humans and as Christians, as beings made in the image of God, to participate in God's leadership.

This brings us to the foundational truth that we will be pursuing through the following chapters, a truth that underlies all we are saying about what leadership means: All true leadership is a participation in the leadership of God in Christ through the Holy Spirit. It is of course possible to lead others wrongly, away from God. But this is not real leadership, not leadership founded in the truth. It is rather counterfeit leadership, false leadership, a corruption or a betrayal of our divinely given destiny. This is why we call the way of leading with and in Christ *True Leadership*.

THE NATURE OF OUR TIMES

Given that the world goes forward by the leadership principle, it comes as no surprise that in all times and places human societies have spent much of their energy and resources on leadership formation. The overall health of a society or a civilization can be measured by the quality of its leaders, and by the care it bestows upon their training. A popular way of expressing this is saying that people get the leaders they deserve. A group or a society that understands the nature of leadership and takes it seriously will tend to produce leaders who reflect that understanding. A group or a society who take leadership lightly or who have a corrupted understanding of it will tend to produce corrupt and deficient leaders.

We are living in a time of crisis in leadership. Even a brief look at the current state of both the Church and the wider society will yield the conclusion, first, that this is a time when good leadership is especially important, and second, that we are facing grave failures in leadership.

Every age needs good leaders. But in times of fundamental social stability, when long-standing arrangements and regard for tradition impart a general wisdom to the whole of a society, failures in leadership, while harmful, do not necessarily lead to immediate disaster. The force of custom and the strength of societal institutions can cover a multitude of leadership sins, as they are meant to do. Our time is not like that. There are many factors that make our age unique. Such factors include rapid change and the increasing complexity of life, the growth of new technologies and their effect on our social and personal lives, an emerging and unprecedented interrelatedness in politics and economics and social customs across the globe, and a dissolving of tradition and a general contempt for the customs of the past, along with an arrogant confidence on the part of many who think that we are fully capable of solving our problems with our own resources. Our time is not one for sleepy leadership. We need to be wide awake. All our basic institutions, from family to business and professional life to Church governance, are in the process of transformation, and at times are tottering under concerted attack. Serious moral challenges have arisen in ways not faced before: the biomedical revolution and the astounding possibilities it opens stands as an example of many such challenges. The very concept of what it means to be human is up for grabs. If ever there was a time when good leadership was necessary—clear-headed and strong-charactered leadership—that time is ours.

In the face of these stiff challenges, in the midst of this swirling change accompanied by the possibility of either major strides forward or massive setback, can we point with confidence to our leaders? Do those who seek out positions of leadership seem equipped for the challenge? Or on the contrary do we see a lamentable lack of clear and effective leadership? Little wonder that people's confidence in their leaders in all spheres of life is at a very low ebb.

This failure of leadership has little to do with a lack of technical skill. Never in history have there been so many experts so well-trained in so many fields. The failure is elsewhere, and twofold: it is first a failure of *vision*, an inability to seize opportunities and to forestall potential dangers because of a lack of a compelling understanding of the nature of our times, whose deepest wounds are those of the mind; and secondly it is a failure of *character*, a paralysis of will resulting from the enervating effects of pride, affluence, and comfort, a failure in the courage and self-control, endurance and selflessness that true leadership demands. This can be seen most clearly in the all-too-common abdication of parental leadership and the destruction of family life, which is the nursery of all true leadership.

It is also seen in the larger worlds of politics and business, education and the Church. The tabloid stories of such failures flashing constantly across the electronic globe are only the most titillating examples of an epidemic that has gripped the whole of the society. At the same time, though our situation is serious, there is great promise. A large and growing number of our youth are eager to shoulder responsibility in leadership. Many among them have an intuitive understanding of the needs of our time. Many have a genuine and growing love for Christ and his Church. Many want their lives to be characterized by wisdom and heroism. Yet moved as they are by high ideals, they are often ill-equipped for the challenges that await them. They can suffer from a lack of vision concerning the nature of true leadership or from a weak and ill-formed character. The world they have grown up in—self-indulgent, aimless, and distracted as it tends to be—is a poor training ground for good leadership. This can give rise to discouragement and cynicism in the face of failure. Many among them are looking for guidance, for help in identifying the task before them and for the formation of mind and will to enable them to meet the challenge of that task.

These observations point to a situation that is at once sobering and promising: sobering in that it calls for a decisive response in the face of pressing need; promising in that much can be accomplished among and by the coming generation in helping to heal the wounds of our time, if young men and women who are stepping forward can be equipped to meet the challenge before them. This book is meant to be a contribution toward the fulfillment of that promise.

TRUE LEADERSHIP

— NOTES —

CHAPTER 2

≈   ≈

WHAT IS TRUE LEADERSHIP?

He who has never learned to obey cannot be a good commander.
ARISTOTLE

*Do you wish to rise? Begin by descending. You plan a tower that will
pierce the clouds? Lay first the foundation of humility.*
ST. AUGUSTINE

*And Jesus called them to him and said to them, "You know that those
who are supposed to rule over the Gentiles lord it over them, and their
great men exercise authority over them. But it shall not be so among
you; but whoever would be great among you must be your servant, and
whoever would be first among you must be slave of all. For the Son of
Man also came not to be served but to serve, and to give his life as a
ransom for many."*
MARK 10:42–45

LEADERSHIP IS A much-discussed term and can mean many different
things. So we need a working definition of true leadership. True leadership is:

≈   13

1. A participation in the leadership of Jesus Christ,
2. Involving the exercise of influence,
3. That moves others toward goodness and the Kingdom of God,
4. That respects the proper dignity of those being led,
5. That works through the whole spiritual and moral being of the leader, and
6. That is normally exercised in the context of commonly shared institutional life.

Let us now examine each aspect of this definition in more detail.

1. *True leadership is a participation in the leadership of Jesus Christ.*

This foundational principle was noted in Chapter One. It is worth reminding ourselves of it continually, because it provides the key to understanding the rest. There is one leader of the human race, the God-man Jesus Christ. Christians acknowledge this when they call him Lord. Many scriptural descriptions of Christ point to this truth. He is ruler, master, the one who bears authority, "upholding the universe by his word of power" (Heb 1:3). "He is the head of the body, the church; he is the beginning, the first-born from the dead, that in everything he might be pre-eminent" (Col 1:18). He is the one who "opens and no one shall shut, who shuts and no one opens" (Rev 3:7). He is the one before whom every knee will bend, and whom every tongue will call Lord (Phil 2:10–11). When the Mexican Cristeros, facing down the firing squads, shouted out "Viva Cristo Rey!" they were proclaiming this reality. Christ is King. He is the Leader.

But this does not end the matter. Because we are created in God's image, because we are "in Christ," members of his body in communion with him, because we have become "partakers of the divine nature" (2 Pet 1:4), we participate in his life and in his work. He shares a portion of his kingly authority with us. He brings us into his leadership. He does not do this by setting us up on our own as mini-kinglets; he gives us both more and less than that. He gives us less, in that we exercise no leadership that is simply "ours." Everything that we do as leaders is derivative of another, of Christ. He gives us more, in that our leadership is not bound by our own limitations and is not upheld by our own meager efforts. "He who receives any one whom I send receives me; and he who receives me receives him who sent me," said Jesus to his disciples (Jn 13:20). Christ himself inhabits our leadership. It is his, and it is ours. It is ours *because* it is his and because we belong to him. The true leader understands leadership to be founded on Christ's words: "He who abides in me, and I in him, he it is that bears much fruit, for apart from me you can do nothing" (Jn 15:5). The true leader knows that apart from Christ he or she can do, literally, nothing; nothing that will be of lasting value for the leadership of the human race. At the same time the true leader can say with Paul, "I can do all things in him who strengthens me" (Phil 4:13). Nothing apart from Christ, everything with him: these are the two poles of True Leadership.

2. *True leadership is the exercise of influence.*

Leadership often involves a specific title or position, but that is not the whole story. Many who lead effectively have no explicit position. Those who do have leadership positions may not be leaders in any particular sense. More important for the leader even than a position or a title is the exercise of influence. Who are those who can and do exercise such influence? Parents, pastors, employers, teachers, politicians, friends, writers or artists, fellow humans. Any or all of these may lead truly.

A true leader is a person with a certain weight, who moves whatever situation he or she enters in good directions. We all know this quality when we are in its presence. Its possessor does not need to be a particular personality type or hold a specific title. Rather there is something weighty in the person's way of being, expressed in words and actions and general bearing, but transcending all of them. In the presence of this kind of weight, things go differently: conversations take a different turn, goodness flourishes, evil subsides, all without the knowledge of the one who is making so profound a difference.

The question might be posed: Who has been the most influential leader in history? Who has transformed the world most? Whose life has made the most difference in others' thought and action? Possible candidates crowd the mind: statesmen and conquerors, prophets and teachers of religion, scientists and inventors, artists and writers. Setting aside Christ himself, (who on any reckoning has to be at the top of such a list, but who has the advantage of being the incarnate Son of God), where might the choice land? A good case could be made, on empirical grounds alone, that history's most influential leader has been Mary, the mother of Jesus. Consider how universally she has been honored and remembered and thought of; how often her example has given hope and inspiration to countless people of all walks of life; how many minds and hearts have been changed through her influence. Yet she never had an earthly title or position. She is perhaps the purest example of what it means to properly exercise influence.

Later we will consider what constitutes such weight, a quality mainly rooted in character. For now we might note a particular temptation of our time, a temptation that the ancients called pusillanimity and that might be described as timidity in exercising influence. The temptation says: "Don't make waves; don't have strong convictions; play it safe; fit in; the middle of the road is the smart place to be." To the degree that such sentiments dominate a person's attitude to life, that person will not be leading. According to the old saying, "only a dead fish goes with the flow." This spineless attitude is sometimes graced with positive-sounding names like tolerance and niceness. But such niceness and such tolerance are often only cleverly disguised calculations to dodge the inconvenience of responsibility and the unpleasantness of conflict. Jesus, the model leader whose attitude toward others was a perfect model of selflessness and goodness, did not avoid conflict and confrontation where it was called for. He was not "nice" in the often-debased meaning of that word. He was something much nobler and more challenging, as well as more influential: he was loving; he was motivated by charity. He calls all those who participate in his leadership to the same influential character.

3. *True leadership moves others toward goodness and the Kingdom of God.*

True leadership, leadership in Christ, always moves others toward God, which is to say toward all things good and true and beautiful, toward the coming of the Kingdom.

An effective and dynamic person who exercises a great deal of influence, but does so in a way that leads away from goodness and truth and God, is not a true leader, but rather a false one. The prime example of this kind of false leadership is that exercised by the enemy of the human race, the Prince of Darkness.

Jesus calls the devil "the father of lies." The devil possesses an admittedly overwhelming personality. He wields a great deal of influence, and by his clever malice he leads many astray. He is effective, but untrue. Those who take their cue from him, often without knowing it—talented people in politics, in education, in music and the arts, in family life, not least, in the Church—are not true leaders, but rather counterfeits. They are using for bad ends what was put into their hands for good purposes. Leadership, which has its origin in God, always leads toward life and goodness, toward "whatever is true, whatever is honorable, whatever is just, whatever is pure, whatever is lovely, whatever is gracious, if there is any excellence, if there is anything worthy of praise" (Phil 4:8). To the degree that leadership runs away from such goodness, it has run away from its source in God and has been corrupted by selfishness.

In the exercise of leadership there will always be a mixture of good and bad. Even the worst of people are not bad or wrong in everything, and the best are never entirely free of flaws and failures. This means that those who are growing into true leaders need to engage in a continual process of self-purification; to be trained, with God's help, in habits of goodness. It is often the case that the most dangerous of false leaders are those who are half-true, and therefore confusing and seductive. The heretic is more dangerous than the open unbeliever. The person who constantly speaks in the language of high moral ideals but who influences others toward darkness is more likely to exercise evil influence than the scoffing cynic.

4. *True leadership respects the proper dignity of those it leads.*
True leadership acknowledges the dignity of those being led, and increases that dignity by its exercise. The art of true leadership is not the skill of getting people to do what we want by whatever means. It is not a secret technique to win friends and influence people. It is not cajolery or mindless propaganda. It is not emotional blackmail. It is not the attempt to control or dominate or manipulate others by appealing to their fear or lust or greed. It is not flattery. It is not self-aggrandizement and the imposition of our will upon others. All these deformations of true leadership, often subtle in their operation, harm the dignity of those being led.

True leadership involves an honest appeal to the mind and the will, the highest faculties of our nature. It addresses itself to what is true and what is good. It prefers to lose influence rather than to gain it by sacrificing the dignity and the humanity of those being led. In this the true leader imitates Christ, the perfect leader.

Anyone who looks carefully at the life of Jesus in the Gospels must be struck by how honest he is toward those he leads. He never flatters his followers in order to gain attention or loyalty. He rather tells them the truth about themselves even when it is not easy to hear. He doesn't entice them by an appeal to walk an easy road; instead he seemingly puts obstacles in their way: "Blessed are you when men revile you and persecute you and utter all kinds of evil against you falsely on my account" (Mt 5:11). He does not compromise his teaching to allow for human weakness: rather, his directions are very challenging: love your enemies, turn the other cheek, do not look lustfully, do not be angry with your brother (Mt 6). When crowds attracted by his impressive miracles begin to run after him, he confronts them with the horror of crucifixion (Mk 8:34). When many leave him, dismayed by his teaching concerning the eating and drinking of his body and blood, he does not soften his words, but lets those who will, go (Jn 6). Had Jesus hired a good public relations consultant and done some solid marketing research, perhaps he could have avoided these problems. But it was not his intention to avoid them. He never altered the content of his teaching to suit the expectations of his hearers. He was concerned that those who came to him came for the right reasons. He wanted true followers who had counted the cost, not hangers-on who were momentarily excited. He wanted sons and daughters, not slaves. He wanted genuine friends who had chosen to follow him freely by a straight-forward appeal to what was good and true, not wide-eyed devotees captivated or seduced by marvels. This attitude of Jesus, difficult and even harsh though it can sometimes seem, confers great dignity on those who follow him. He teaches them their full humanity by the manner of his leadership.

Paul speaks of his own leadership in the same terms: "We have renounced disgraceful, underhanded ways; we refuse to practice cunning or to tamper with God's word, but by the open statement of the truth we would commend ourselves to every man's conscience in the sight of God" (2 Cor 4:2–3).

An important principle underlies the concern of Jesus to protect the dignity of those he was leading, and applies to all who exercise leadership: the good of the immortal souls we lead is always more important than any immediate practical goal we may have in mind. The ultimate point of our life on earth, and therefore the ultimate point of all true leadership, is that we might be changed, transformed into creatures worthy of union with God; that we might learn self-emptying love and so come into the fullness of our humanity, ready to embrace an eternal destiny. For this to happen our minds and our wills need to be healed and properly trained, and the exercise of true leadership furthers this process.

Parents are rightly concerned for an ordered family life, for a clean house and a well-kept yard, for teaching their children obedience and insisting they get along with one another. But these good goals need to be achieved in a way that brings those children a greater measure of maturity and genuine love. If family order were accomplished through a regime of terror, or by administering drugs, or by bribes and favors that led to habits of self-indulgence, such leadership would defeat its proper purpose.

A businessman reasonably wants to see his company flourish and make a profit. But if he accomplished this by creating an atmosphere of excessive anxiety, or by paying employees less than a fair wage, or by forcing them to work unreasonable hours to the detriment of their family life and religious obligations, or by practicing deceit or false advertising on those who were buying his products, he would have failed in his first duty.

A politician is rightly concerned for a smoothly running civic life. But if this were attained only under the iron hand of an oppressive police state, or by playing upon fear or greed rather than appealing to reason and justice, or by giving advantage to the powerful and ignoring the weak, such a person would be a failure as a leader.

A missionary is properly motivated by the desire for conversions. But if converts were gained by highlighting attractive aspects of the faith and hiding difficult ones, or by exercising a self-oriented charm that led others to honor the one preaching rather than the One who was the point of the preaching, or by inflaming the social or political or religious prejudices of those listening, this would be an expression of false, not true leadership. True leadership is always measured with the human in mind, and always confers dignity on those being led.

5. *True leadership works through the whole spiritual and moral being of the leader.*

Leadership is a habit, a way of being, a quality that inheres in the personality, not a knack or a technique. It involves skills, but it is not mainly a skill. It is a fundamental human activity, rooted in our creation in the likeness of God, which is why everyone has some measure of ability for it. True leadership is not so much what a person does; it is who that person is. If someone is a leader, that person exercises influence all the time, often unwittingly, in ways that vary according to the changing needs and roles of life.

As was noted earlier, explicit leadership positions do not and cannot make a leader. Such positions are important and necessary, and provide the context and scope for the exercise of leadership; but they are no substitute for it. True leadership is attained and possessed as an expression of a person's character. Those who use positions of leadership to compensate for what they lack within themselves always make a hash of their leadership duties. Many people have children; fewer are true fathers and mothers. Many attain positions of authority in business or politics or the Church or civic life; fewer exercise true leadership. Everyone has had the miserable experience of suffering through the supposed leadership of a weak-charactered or unprincipled person whose failures led to all manner of difficulties.

Because leadership is rooted in the spiritual and moral being of the person, true leadership can be attained only slowly. It isn't gained simply by attending a weekend seminar or reading a book, or by completing a certification process or getting an advanced degree, good and helpful as such things may be. It is forged in the inner being of the person; it is the fruit of long training, of seriously engaging the fight against self, of wrestling with the many individual decisions in the challenge of life, all with the help of God. There is no short cut to attaining it.

This is one reason why family life is so important for the health of any human society and for the proper training of leaders. Only in a family context can the combination of personal concern, training over a course of years, and ties of affection and loyalty be found. Other institutions such as schools and seminaries and summer camps share these duties, but they do so most effectively by imitating and building on family life. The long process necessary to gain strong character also explains the reluctance of much of the leadership world to seriously tackle the challenge of true leadership. It is easier to advertise a "life-changing weekend" that communicates a set of superficial skills than to help people set out on the years-long task of forging character.

6. *True leadership is normally exercised in the context of common institutional life.*

The institutional aspect of true leadership, often misunderstood or neglected, is so important that it deserves a longer treatment of its own in a later chapter. For now it is enough to say that true leadership is not a solitary affair, and unless we understand the nature and the purpose of institutions in human life, we will have a hard time understanding what it means to lead well and truly.

THE MEANING OF SERVANT LEADERSHIP

It is striking that the one who genuinely possesses authority, who is by nature and by right the leader and ruler of humanity, God himself made man, came among us as one who serves. All who participate in his leadership need to take the same posture. To lead is to serve, to put the interests of others ahead of our own.

The notion of servant leadership has been attractive in recent years and has gained a good measure of merited attention. It will help, in clarifying and embracing this concept, to see the manner in which Christ was a servant.

The first and most important service Christ performed for others was to do the will of his heavenly Father. "For I have come down from heaven," he said, "not to do my own will, but the will of him who sent me" (Jn

6:38). In determining how he was to deal with the various people and the situations he encountered, his first thought was to look to another, to the Father, and to act according to his Father's direction. For Jesus, to lead was to follow. He led others by following the Father. He served those around him, his family, his disciples, the crowds who came to hear him, the blind and lame and sick, ultimately the whole human race, by keeping his eyes on the Father and doing the Father's will. As with love, so with service, we are oriented first to God, then to others. These two aspects of service, to God and to others, are not in conflict with one another. Just as the call to love God with one's whole heart is the ground from which genuine love of neighbor springs, so our service to others will find both its source and its direction in our service to God. What was true for Jesus is doubly true for any who follow in his footsteps. The first duty of the true leader is to serve the True Leader. To lead is to follow.

Remembering this principle of leading and following can help us avoid a possible pitfall in leadership. To be a servant leader means to serve others as Christ would, according to the mind of God. It does not mean to be a butler-leader, who simply does the will of others. Yet if service to God is not at the forefront, it is easy for those who lead to serve others in ways that do not genuinely help them. The moment when Jesus's service to his disciples looked most "butlerish" (or rather was beneath what any self-respecting butler would have done), saw Jesus still insisting on the Father's will. At the Last Supper the disciples watched their beloved rabbi and revered teacher stoop to the lowest kind of menial task, one usually performed by a slave, and wash their feet. It was an important lesson concerning the right attitude of the leader toward those he serves. But even then, Jesus was not simply putting himself at the pleasure of his followers. He did not ask them what they wanted him to do for them. Quite the opposite, it was evidently difficult for them to receive the service he was providing, and Peter went so far as to refuse it. At that point Jesus made clear that this was the Father's will, and Peter needed to submit to it if he wanted any part in God. It is an interesting encounter: the one who has taken the part of a lowly slave is giving orders to the one he is serving.

This principle can be seen most clearly in parental leadership, which is the foundational model of all true leadership. Parents serve their children in many and irreplaceable ways; it is one of the great tasks of their vocation. But serving their children seldom means doing what their children want them to do. They serve them as much by disciplining them as they do by granting their requests. Their goal is to be of true help to them, and that can only be gauged by keeping true to another's direction. Parents who lead their children truly do not say to them (in so many words): "We are in charge, so do what we say because we are the ones to be obeyed." Nor do they say, "You are in charge, so tell us what you want and we will serve you." They say rather: "We are following another, the true leader of us all. Come follow us as we follow him; *he* is the one to be obeyed." If this attitude gets lost, parental authority can become arbitrary and difficult for children to respect. And parents who don't like the idea of tyrannizing over their children, but who have no direction for their leadership that comes from following another, can abdicate their position and effectively be led by the very children they are supposedly leading.

The same can happen in any exercise of leadership. As Aristotle pointed out, the first requirement for the good leader is to be a good follower.

∴ ∴ ∴

If all true leadership is a participation in the leadership of Jesus Christ, then before spelling out in greater detail the features and foundations of true leadership, something needs to be said about what it means that Christ is the leader of the human race.

What Is True Leadership?

— NOTES —

CHAPTER 3

CHRIST THE LEADER
AND THE UTOPIAN TEMPTATION

We are the world; we are the children; we are the ones to make a brighter day, so let's start giving. We've a choice we're making; we're saving our own lives. It's true we'll make a better day, just you and me.
MICHAEL JACKSON *&* LIONEL RITCHIE

In the days of those kings the God of heaven will set up a kingdom which shall never be destroyed, nor shall its sovereignty be left to another people. It shall break in pieces all these kingdoms and bring them to an end, and it shall stand forever.
DANIEL 2:44

THE IMPORTANCE OF THE KINGDOM

Here is no idea more common to the New Testament than that of "the Kingdom." When John the Baptist preached the imminent coming of Christ, he called his hearers to repent, to change, "for the Kingdom of Heaven is at hand" (Mt 3:2). Jesus took up the same phrase; Matthew gives a summary description of his activity: "He went about all Galilee, teaching in their synagogues and preaching the gospel of the Kingdom and healing every disease and every infirmity among the people" (Mt 4:23). In the Beatitudes Jesus referred to the Kingdom of Heaven as the highest of blessings: those who were poor in spirit, who were persecuted for righteousness, would receive it (Mt 5:3, 10). He said that one needed to be born again to enter this Kingdom (Jn 3:3). He cast out demons as a sign of the Kingdom's coming (Mt 12:28). He taught his followers that they needed to be childlike to inherit the Kingdom (Lk 18:17). He said that the rich would enter the Kingdom only with difficulty (Lk 18:25). He assigned the Kingdom to his disciples (Lk 22:29), and told many parables about what it would be like (cf. Mt 13; Lk 13). At his crucifixion he made a promise to the repentant thief who then asked Jesus to remember him when he came into his Kingdom (Lk 23:42). "Thy Kingdom come" is a key petition in the prayer he taught his disciples. And the triumphant praise sung in heaven at the end of time rejoices that "the kingdom of the world has become the Kingdom of our Lord and of his Christ, and he shall reign forever and ever" (Rev 11:15). The establishment of this Kingdom fulfills the prophecy from the book of Daniel noted at the head of the chapter, one that was echoed by many other passages from the Hebrew prophets: God himself would set up a kingdom that would eventually bring under its rule the whole of the human race.

There is much concerning the meaning of the Kingdom that goes beyond the scope of this discussion. What is relevant to our topic is that the notion of a kingdom implies authority and rule, or to use a more modern term, leadership. The drama of the human race is a drama of contested authority, a dispute over who is rightful leader of humanity. That drama is summed up in the second Psalm: "The kings of the earth set themselves, and the rulers take counsel together, against the Lord and his anointed, saying, 'Let us burst their bonds asunder, and cast their cords from us.' He who sits in the heavens laughs; the Lord has them in derision. Then he will speak to them in his wrath, and terrify them in his fury, saying, 'I have set my king on Zion, my holy hill.'" It is the tragedy of our race and the source of all our suffering that we have turned from the one who is rightful ruler, one whose rule brings life and freedom, and have attempted to set ourselves in his place. In Christian understanding, we call this tragedy the Fall. It colors the whole of our history, both communal and individual.

CHRIST AS THE KING

The Gospels tell the remarkable story of the manner by which God determined to reverse the Fall and to establish his eternal kingdom among humans, and they reveal the extraordinary personality of the one called Christ who bears God's rule. They recount the deeds of a king who won back his kingdom not by violent conquest, but by a loving appeal to truth; who entered into his inheritance through toil and suffering; who walked among his subjects shorn of the outward trappings of authority; and who, though superior to them in every respect, took the position of a servant among them. They tell of the establishment of a kingdom that was genuinely in this world, but that transcended the world, a kingdom that would maintain its sway over its subjects not by coercion but by entering into their willing minds and hearts. They tell the previously unthinkable tale of how the eternal God united himself to the human race in order to save us from the disastrous results of our rebellion. All of this is unspeakably good news.

There is an important point to remember in this good news. Though Christ comes humbly, and seeks out followers by a free appeal to mind and will, he is nonetheless the leader, the rightful ruler of the human race. Though he does not (yet) demand or coerce obedience, it is his task to set right the ills of the world and to bring all of creation to its rightful allegiance. Paul speaks of the future time when Christ "delivers the kingdom to God the Father after destroying every rule and every authority and power. For he must reign until he has put all his enemies under his feet" (1 Cor 15:24–25). Many scriptural designations of Christ point to this truth: he is the new Adam, the firstborn of all creation, the alpha and omega, the heir of all things, the King of kings and Lord of lords. Because he is God himself, the Word of God united to humanity, all authority, all leadership is his. This brings us back once more to our foundational principle: all true leadership is a participation in the leadership of Jesus Christ.

This does not mean that Christ is simply the strongest and most forceful of powers, the "top dog" who bends all other wills to his. God is unlike any other being; he is not one among them, but rather the ground of the existence of all that is. "In him we live and move and have our being" (Acts 17:28). To be rightly ordered to the will of God is not to be oppressed by a superior power; it is to enter into a communion of love apart from which we can never find freedom and life. There is no "zero sum game" here: the rule of Christ does not stifle us or limit our potential; it is the atmosphere within which our minds and wills breathe a free and healthy air and our potentialities find their rightful fulfillment. The greater one's fidelity to Christ's rule, the more truly one's life will be lived.

What this means—that Christ is leader of the human race—can be seen more clearly against the backdrop of a common temptation of our time: the desire to save the world apart from the mind and the action of God.

THE UTOPIAN TEMPTATION

No one doubts that the world is in great need of "fixing." Whether one looks to the material order where poverty and disease afflict so many, or to the political world characterized too often by injustice and oppression and corruption, or to the inner world of loneliness and hatred and broken relationships, it is clear that something has gone very wrong with the human race and needs to be set right. Christians understand the source of the problem to be a fundamental turning away from God that has deeply wounded our inner nature and delivered the world to the power of darkness and vanity. They realize the depth of that wound, and the impossibility of its healing by anything humans can do on their own. Nonetheless they are full of hope, because the one Being who has the knowledge and the power to address the situation, to "fix" the world, God himself, has determined to do it, and is even now in the process of putting things right. As a result, Christians are full of energy for the genuine betterment of the human race. But they know that if one wants to make things better, the first question one asks is: "What is God in Christ doing?" That One who has perfect knowledge of the world and its ills, and perfect love as his animating principle, enlists the participation of any who will work with him for the saving and the healing of the race. His diagnosis of the problem and his prescriptions for its solution are accurate and completely effective, and they are the only way to successfully address humanity's problems.

Since the arrival of the intellectual and social movement that came to flower in the eighteenth century and goes by the name of "Enlightenment," a great revolution in the attitude of our society has taken place concerning the solution to the ills of the world. The leaders of the Enlightenment, greatly taken with the advances their civilization had made materially and socially, and looking forward to ever greater mastery of the physical environment through the progress of applied sciences, lost sight of the real nature of humanity's wound. They denied the Fall, and insisted that our real enemy was ignorance, whether of physical laws or social dynamics or psychological principles. They thought that by properly mastering and applying these various branches of knowledge they could end the suffering of humanity and construct a kind of heaven on earth. They believed, in the words of Nicholas Condorcet, a Frenchman who wrote at the end of the eighteenth century and whose writings provide a neat summary of the ideas of the Enlightenment, that "the perfectibility of man is indefinite." Nurtured by evolutionary philosophies, the idea gained ground that the human race was on an inevitable upward course, and a future of happiness and comfort awaited us if only we would take the task properly in hand.

This idea in various forms came to dominate the life of our society, so much so that the ideology of progress may be called the working religion of the modern age.

For those of this cast of mind, Christianity was a serious problem. By putting their hope in a new heaven and a new earth yet to come, Christians were thought to divert energy and attention from what the Enlighteners considered the real task, which was to fix the earth as it was here and now. The Christian insistence on the reality of the Fall and the impossibility of healing its effects apart from the action of God was felt to be a pernicious doctrine that held humanity in check. Enlightenment thought took exception to the attitude of G. K. Chesterton, who in response to a London newspaper's invitation to write an essay on the topic "What's Wrong With the World?" famously penned his two-word answer: "I am." *The Humanist Manifesto*, written in 1933 largely by noted American educational thinker John Dewey, put it this way: "We can discover no divine purpose or providence for the human species. While there is much that we do not know, humans are responsible for what we are or will become. No deity will save us; we must save ourselves."

No God will save us; we must save ourselves. This is the attitude that we are here calling the utopian temptation. Utopia is a term first coined by the Englishman Thomas More. It comes from the Greek word for "nowhere." It refers to the belief that we can overcome all our problems by the application of our own minds and resources; that there is no fundamental flaw or wound at the root of our difficulties beyond our capacity to handle; that the world will become an ever better place through our own energy, not just materially, but also morally and socially. Most modern ideologies have a utopian core. Marxist communism is utopian; nationalist fascism is utopian; the movement for sexual liberation is utopian; the green movement is utopian; those who think science will solve all our problems are utopians; those who think American capitalist democracy is the answer to all the world's ills are utopians.

Whatever might be the genuine insights of these various ideologies, they are always built on the same bit of sand: the claim to address the ills of the world apart from the cooperation of God. The truth is, we have all become utopians to some degree, even Christians, though we should know better. It is an attractive temptation: utopian dreams are expressed in high-sounding and compelling moral language, and our technical prowess has given us remarkable power to effect change in certain limited areas of human life. Yet the temptation is dangerous. Utopians deny a basic aspect of our reality, namely that the reason evil dominates the world is because individual humans are captured by evil in ways they cannot escape on their own. As a result, every utopian scheme identifies an erroneous source for the obvious darkness in the world. Rather than looking within the individual human heart, utopians look outward, and find there the true cause of evil: the aristocracy, or the reactionaries, or the bourgeoisie, or the Jews, or the liberals, or the inferior races, or the upholders of patriarchy, or white hegemonists, or the homophobes, or the over-populators. Whoever the targeted group happens to be, they are seen to have placed themselves athwart progress and now stand in the way of the fulfillment of the human race. If only they could be bypassed, the world would go on merrily. They therefore need to be resisted and if necessary done away with. However high-sounding the rhetoric, utopian movements always end by killing people. Modern utopians are the great mass murderers of history, and the death toll continues to mount. We should not be surprised at this. If those who had no medical knowledge confidently stepped forward and began operating on people's brains, the likely result would be serious harm. If those who have a profoundly erroneous understanding of human nature and its true ills begin operating on human society, things will necessarily go sadly awry.

CHRIST'S DIAGNOSIS OF THE ILLS OF THE WORLD

Jesus often used the image of himself as a doctor. "Those who are well have no need of a physician, but those who are sick; I came not to call the righteous, but sinners" (Mk 2:17). His many miraculous physical cures were an external expression of a more profound inner operation. At the heart of the good news of Christianity is the consoling truth that when God came among us, he came not to judge our sins, but rather to heal their effects. St. Augustine once noted that the Scriptures often say that God will destroy his enemies. Yes, said Augustine; but God's preferred way of accomplishing this, the most decisive destruction possible, is by turning his enemies into his friends. What then is Christ's diagnosis? What is the road back to our true dignity, the path to re-finding ourselves as God's friends?

When the divine physician looked at his patient, he was confronted by three serious problems. First there was our rebellion to deal with: not only the claims of justice demanding that evil be rightly punished, but the deep wound we had inflicted upon ourselves by our willful separation from the source of goodness, leaving us in a conflicted and chaotic inner state. We desired good as beings created in the image of God, but we had a fatal tendency toward evil in the daily matters of life. Second, by our sin we had delivered ourselves into the power of the enemy of the human race, that angelic being who had rebelled against God, and in his envy of the high destiny of humanity had determined to enslave the creatures he was meant to serve. Third, there was the whole of human society, meant for good but now dominated by sinful humans under the influence of darkness, and tending to enshrine pride, injustice, violence, greed, and lust as its working principles. The classic Christian expression of this state of things, of these enemies of human happiness, is found in the traditional triad: the world, the flesh, and the devil. In this formulation can be seen God's diagnosis of our ills. How would humanity's physician address these three conditions that between them had locked us into our tragic course?

The first task was to break the hold of the devil upon the human race. As Bilbo Baggins once sagely said, "It does not do to leave a live dragon out of your calculations, if you live near him." Jesus knew that attempting to aid the human race without "binding the strong man" was the worst sort of futility. "The devil took him up, and showed him all the kingdoms of the world in a moment of time, and said to him, 'To you I will give all this authority and their glory; for it has been delivered to me, and I give it to whom I will'" (Lk 4:6). This episode from the temptation of Christ makes clear who the ruler of fallen humanity was. That leadership Christ contested and overthrew. This is why casting out demons had such a prominent place in his ministry. It was a sign that in Christ the human race had been given the authority to defy and conquer its former tyrannical overlord. When the disciples of Jesus returned to him marveling that they too could cast out demons, Jesus said to them: "I saw Satan fall like lighting from heaven. Behold, I have given you authority to tread upon serpents and scorpions, and over all the power of the enemy; and nothing shall hurt you" (Lk 10:18–19). By this proclamation of our freedom, Christ showed that he had dealt with enemy number one for those who followed him.

The second task was to restore humanity to its original purity and to wipe out the stain of our sin. Here we touch on the heart of the Christian faith, about which the whole Christian world constantly speaks. Enough for us to say that by his suffering and by offering himself as a sacrificial victim, Christ regained our innocence, and by rising from the dead and sending the Holy Spirit upon his disciples he began the work of healing the wound in our inner being and of bringing us to our full and true humanity, a work of mercy that continues in the life of the Church he founded. This renewed innocence and the gift of divine life is made available to all who are willing to put aside their former rebellion and come back to their rightful king, to their true allegiance.

The third task was to deal with "the world," created in goodness but now enmeshed in patterns of sin and darkness. This task came third, because it would not make sense to think about building a society infused with goodness until the power of the ruler of this world had been dealt with, and the inner wound of humanity had begun to be addressed. During his short stay among us, Christ did not set up humanitarian organizations for the material and social betterment of the world. However excellent their aims, such endeavors could make little difference until the sources of our evil were dealt with. Christ did not come among us just to "make the world a better place." Such a phrase implies a utopian vision; it suggests that things are good but not good enough; that a little effort here and there will do the job; that what the world needs is enhancement and adjustment. Knowing the depth of our true need, Christ came with a nobler and a sterner purpose. He came to end spiritual slavery, to forgive sin, and to renew creation from the ground up, in each individual person and in humanity as a whole. He came to bring a dead race back to life. He then instructed his followers in the Church to influence the world; to use their energy and creativity to help build, in the phrase of Pope Saint John Paul II, a civilization of love.

True leadership is founded on these realities. It begins with the truth of who we are, of who God is, of what our true state is, and of what God is doing about it. Those who wish to make a difference through their leadership, whatever the context, will need to follow the prescriptions given us by Christ, our true physician. They will want to find out how to participate in Christ's leadership. They will need to resist the utopian temptation, not because they don't care about the state of the human race, but precisely because they care about it so much.

Christ the Leader and the Utopian Temptation

— NOTES —

PART II

The Five Foundations of True Leadership

~ CHAPTER 4 ~

THE FIRST FOUNDATION OF TRUE LEADERSHIP: CHRISTIAN CONVICTION

"Who Am I Following?"

In this trying time...we Catholics, and especially we students, have a serious duty to fulfill: our self-formation.
BLESSED PIER GIORGIO FRASSATI

The love of Christ controls us.
2 CORINTHIANS 5:14

THE FIVE FOUNDATIONS OF TRUE LEADERSHIP

What are the requirements, the building blocks, for the attainment of true leadership? What does it take to be a true leader, and how does one get there? We have identified five essential aspects of true leadership, which, though related to one another and resulting in a unified character, can still be examined separately. In the order of their importance the five foundations are: (1) Christian conviction; (2) character; (3) vocation; (4) gifts; and (5) skills. Ranking them this way turns a good deal of current leadership literature on its head. Almost everyone who deals with leadership begins at the bottom of the list—with skills. The more involved treatments go on to speak of gifts. Some dabble in questions of vocation and point to certain aspects of character, but not usually in a systematic way.

Faith, Christian conviction, is usually left out of the picture, or if referred to, is vaguely addressed as the need for some higher purpose. Our approach to leadership is different. We have begun with faith and have put character in the second place as the two indispensable foundations of true leadership. Once these are understood as primary, vocation, gifts, and skills can find their proper place.

The First Foundation: Christian Conviction

As to the first of these, Christian conviction: Those who have strong conviction will lead with more focus, more intensity, and more endurance. No one can lead others into what they do not believe themselves. Laziness and cynicism and self-interest always defeat good leadership, and tend to corrupt those under their influence. So we can take for granted that good leadership demands a certain determined conviction about what one is leading, whatever the cause or project.

For the Christian leader, a special kind of conviction is necessary. As has been noted, in order to be a true leader, one must first be a true follower. The true leader follows Christ, the one who said, "I came into the world to bear witness to the truth" (Jn 18:37). Because of this, the first requisite is that the true leader be "in Christ," that is, to be serious about being a disciple of Jesus. While this may seem obvious, there is an important corollary to note: one comes into the fullness of true leadership only by the action of God. It is in God, through his Son, by the work of the Holy Spirit, that we attain to this kind of participation. When Peter speaks of our becoming "partakers of the Divine nature" (2 Pet 1), when Paul says that "it is no longer I who live but Christ who lives in me" (Gal 2:20), they are pointing to an amazing truth. Christians, through the free gift of God, are changed from within, and become a different kind of being with divine life coursing through them. So this fact meets us at the beginning of our pursuit of leadership: the most important part of it is a pure gift from God. We cannot determine to be true leaders on our own, as if the source of leadership were somehow within ourselves.

This is not to say that only the Christian can authentically lead. To the degree that a person is following the dictates of reason, tracing God's divine order and attempting to participate in that divine system, such a person will participate in God's leadership as it has come through creation, mediated by conscience and rationality. The principle here is similar to the broader Christian understanding that there is truth to be found in religions and philosophies that are not explicitly Christian. To the degree that the revelation of Christ has clarified and purified human understanding of reality, and has brought divine help to transform that reality, to that degree the Christian has greater possibilities for true leadership.

This is not a treatise on what it means to be a Christian and a Catholic; there are many better places to go for that. Nonetheless, it will help to say something about what it means to bring Christian conviction to our leadership. For that purpose, a look at the traditional scheme of the virtues will be useful. The Church has developed over the centuries a way of understanding and speaking about the life of the Holy Spirit and the form of renewed humanity with the language and theory of the virtues, theological and cardinal.

There are dozens of virtues, strengths of our inner being that become for us a "second nature." These have been gathered in the Church's traditional teaching under seven main virtues: the three theological virtues of faith, hope, and charity, and the four cardinal virtues of prudence, justice, courage, and temperance. The cardinal virtues, first identified and set out by the ancient Greeks, speak to the formation of the character of the good person. They are the so-called natural virtues; they are given us as potentialities when we are created, and in the Christian they are touched by the Holy Spirit and given new strength and vigor. We will look at them when we discuss character. The theological virtues fill out the unique action of the Holy Spirit upon the Christian believer. While a measure of natural virtue is available to every human, the theological virtues of faith, hope, and charity come directly from the hand of God, and are present only by his gift. A look at each in turn will help to clarify for us what it means to say that our Christian conviction is the foundation of our leadership.

FAITH. Faith is the apprehension of reality, especially unseen reality. Faith is the healing of our minds. It enables us to value things according to their proper worth, to see the end of all human affairs, to have a just and proportionate view of events and people. Receiving faith is like being given a new set of eyes by which to see all things as they really are.

At its most elementary level faith involves the recognition that God exists, that he rules the world, and that it is necessary to be in proper relationship to him as a simple practical matter. To go this far is to embrace what the world has always to some degree known. The Roman concern to behave with *pietas*, the Greek recognition that *hubris*, pride toward the gods, would mar the affairs of humans, the Chinese desire to live in harmony with Heaven, all point in this direction. But beyond this natural piety, God has given the world a special revelation concerning his nature, his attitude toward and purposes for the human race, and the means we need to take in order to please him and to come into our true humanity. That revelation comes to us by way of the Jews, God's Chosen People, and is expressed fully in Christ, God incarnate among us in history, by means of the Church he founded. Faith is the apprehension of that revelation and the habit of conforming of our lives to its demands.

To gain faith is to gain the mind of Christ. When we understand the world as Christ did, when we evaluate the honors and riches of the world as Christ did, when we think things important and unimportant as Christ thought them, when we look to our heavenly Father in obedience as Christ did, when we view others as Christ viewed them, when we embrace the life of habitual love and self-control in daily practical matters as Christ did, when we are transformed by the renewal of our minds, we are living by faith.

Faith is not a feeling; it is conviction, the "conviction of things not seen" (Heb 11:1). Faith is not a leap in the dark; it is rather a walk into light. Faith does not contradict what we understand through reason or perceive by our senses; it rather goes beyond them and shows us that which our reason and our senses are not capable of grasping on their own. Faith opens upon us an unseen world centered in God himself, a world that is larger, deeper, richer, more beautiful, more lasting than the one we see. By faith we know that its claims upon us are more important than the material claims of the seen world.

Faith perceives the wound of original sin. It understands that our minds, made to feed upon truth, now tend to darkness and need to be enlightened. It recognizes that we have a blindness to overcome, one that we cannot heal by ourselves. Faith recognizes an immortal soul in every human we meet, a being with a divine purpose and destiny (even if in a distressing disguise of repulsiveness), and therefore worthy of being treated with dignity and justice.

Faith looks to the ultimate end in every beginning. It does not forget that the visible world is passing and often illusory. Faith remembers that we are immortal beings undergoing a test, whose lives have yet to arrive at their definitive form. It keeps the final judgment of the world in view, and evaluates all things in the light of that coming day.

Faith traces the intimate connection between the seen and unseen worlds. It realizes that we reach the unseen by means of the seen, that we travel to the spiritual on the road of the material, that we gain or lose an invisible kingdom on the basis of how we manage the things of time and sense. It therefore takes seriously the material world and honors it, even while giving it secondary importance. Faith sees the Church as belonging to Christ, the body of which he is the head, the temple of his presence, the sacrament that reveals him to the world. In the words of second-century writer Diognetus, it recognizes the Church as the soul of the world. Faith sees the coming of Christ into the world and the offering of his life as the great events of human history around which everything else turns. Faith is the light by which we understand God, ourselves and our world. It is true sight.

Faith is not something we can simply pick up by reading a bestseller, or even train ourselves into. Faith comes from being given a new nature, being changed in our inward being by the action of God. But though a gift, faith is also a habit. The gift comes as a new set of eyes that allow us to perceive the unseen world. But the eye tends to be lazy, and needs training and focus. For this reason we need to develop the habit of faith, which is the constant calling to mind and acting upon what we know to be true. To expect true leadership without a mind renewed by faith is like expecting to fly without wings.

It is unpopular to make this claim in our time, that to be of real use to the world one needs faith. This comes partly because our current world resents the very idea that there might be a special revelation of God, a gift and a grace that some have received and others have not. It is also partly due to the sad fact that so many Christians seem to view the world and behave within it as if they had no supernatural sight whatever, which makes the Christian claim harder to believe. Nonetheless it is true.

The saints are of great importance to us as both practical examples and signs of what God will do with those who come to him sincerely with their entire selves. Saints are those who have taken Christ at his word, and have taken the whole dose of the medicine he offers for the healing of our wounded nature. As a result they see the world more clearly than others, and act upon that sight more consistently. They have a different frame of reference from those around them; they value things according to an accurate heavenly vision rather than a deceptive earthly one. This is not the place for a discussion of how one comes to faith. Here we are only noting this principle: that a true leader needs first to see the world truly in the light of faith. This is the link to reality without which leadership tends to be blind and goes astray.

HOPE. Because we are creatures on the way, not yet in our final form, hope is the necessary atmosphere for our lives. It is also a crucial attribute of the true leader. People can live with a remarkable amount of pain and hardship, provided they have hope. Without hope, even an easy life becomes insupportable. The reason is obvious: present satisfaction will not answer our deepest desires and concerns. We know too well, whether we remember it at every moment or not, that we cannot be happy until we have found a happiness that will not escape us, that will not flit away after a brief moment of satisfaction. We know, deep within ourselves, that we are not yet home, and we will not be content until we are. Hope is the sure confidence that, despite whatever darkness or difficulty may come upon us, despite the grim look of the present moment, we will arrive at our destination and our deepest desires will find fulfillment in God.

Everyone hopes for good things of a finite nature. We hope for health, for a good job, for a good marriage, and happy children. We hope that our favorite team wins, that our financial holdings increase, that there will be good weather for our picnic. The theological virtue of hope goes beyond these limited hopes to what might be called Hope with a capital H. All these other hopes will ultimately fail us and leave us desolate unless we have the ultimate final hope—supernatural hope—hope that at the end of this necessarily transient life we will find completion. An image of such hope is the pregnant woman. She often feels sick; the slender shape that she has spent so much energy preserving has become thick and puffy; her emotions are playing tricks on her; her legs and her back are sore, she gets tired easily, she feels the pain of the baby kicking. All considered, this is not an enviable experience, and it brings with it a good measure of suffering. Yet a pregnant woman is typically not dejected and despairing; quite the reverse. She is filled with plans, she is often happy, she speaks of her suffering with a certain wry humor. People around her smile when they see her even though they know she is in discomfort. The reason is that she and they are looking forward to the birth of her child. She is thinking of a new life and what that new life will mean. She is living in hope. And the very hardships of the pregnancy, the growing burden of the child, are signs that feed her hope.

"This slight momentary affliction is winning for us an eternal weight of glory beyond all comparison" (2 Cor 4:17). So Paul speaks about life as a whole. The point of living in this world is to be born into a new one, and the sufferings and hardships of this time are bringing about the transformation that will make us worthy to receive the life to come. "Suffering produces endurance, and endurance produces character, and character produces hope, and hope does not disappoint us" (Rom 5:4–5).

The true leader is a person of hope, Hope with a capital H. This is not the same as being optimistic, which is often either a particular temperamental quality or even an expression of ignorance. To be a person of hope means taking a posture toward the future that allows an understanding of suffering and setback in the light of the pattern of Christ, that keeps a calm spirit in the midst of difficulty, and that rouses others to endurance and to action in the face of what seem insurmountable obstacles. Those who hope truly, those whose hope is founded in an accurate understanding of where we are headed and by what roads, are not likely to be deceived or bribed or bullied into false and destructive hopes, and are not easily susceptible to losing their courage in the face of seeming failure.

LOVE (CHARITY). Love is so tied to the being of God that John the Apostle can say, "God is love" (1 Jn 4:16). Those who exercise leadership represent the face, the character of God, to those around them. Paul speaks of himself and those working with him as ambassadors of Christ through whom God is making his appeal (2 Cor 5:20). "He who hears you hears me, and he who rejects you rejects me, and he who rejects me rejects him who sent me" (Lk 10:16). So close is the bond between Christ and those through whom he works.

Christ's love was not just an abstract and general love for humanity, which is often a dangerous sentiment, but rather a very particular love for those often timid and sometimes thickheaded and regularly annoying disciples he was training. The love that comes from Christ is universal in its extent, but particular in its object.

The love of Christ, while always life-giving, does not always result in making people feel good or comfortable in the short run. Because God's love is founded in truths that are essential to our welfare, love compels him to insist on those truths even when they are unwelcome. There is much in us that does not want to know the truth about ourselves. We resist taking our proper medicine, and often prefer the momentary comfort of blindness and darkness to the glaring light of truth. Yet love is always related to truth; there can be no love apart from truth. To the degree that we dodge truth, we will be limited in our ability to love.

The love that originates in Christ does not refer to a particular feeling or emotional state. The command that we love our enemies puts that notion to rest: it is impossible to feel good about those who are trying to destroy us. Love, charity, is a settled disposition by which we exercise our will and empty ourselves in favor of the good of another. We cannot compel our emotions; but we can rule our wills and act for the good, with the help of God.

To vary the famous passage from Paul's letter to the Corinthians: *If by my leadership I speak or write in such a way as to exercise influence over multitudes, and move them to great activity, but have not love, I am a noisy gong and a clanging symbol. If I sacrifice and suffer all manner of difficulty in leading, but have not love, I am nothing. If I achieve great success and become famous and all speak well of my leadership, but have not love, I gain nothing.* Love is the very heart of leadership, its center. The true leader is one whose primary motivation is love. Not self-promotion and fame; not power; not wealth; not personal fulfillment and satisfaction; not the hope of leaving a legacy; not the desire to be loved in return; but the genuine good of others. True leadership always looks away from the self.

Once the demands of genuine love are clear, it becomes easier to understand the importance of an inward renewal of life. We are dogged and haunted by self, and the ideal of love set forth in Christ is beyond our own power to achieve. No wonder so many secular philosophers have discarded the Christian understanding of love, and have substituted for it the more attainable ideal of calculated self-interest as the real bond between humans. But the true leader is not daunted by the height of the call. We have hope and courage that comes from beyond us, because "God's love has been poured into our hearts through the Holy Spirit which has been given to us" (Rom 5:5).

⋮ ⋮ ⋮

Faith, hope, and charity make up the Christian conviction of the true leader. They go beyond a mere intellectual assent, and penetrate every aspect of the leader's life. They become the atmosphere in which the true leader lives, the lens and the light by which the true leader sees, the motivating power by which the true leader is animated. They allow the possibility of genuine participation in the leadership of Christ.

— NOTES —

CHAPTER 5

ASSESSING CHRISTIAN CONVICTION

Can a blind man lead a blind man? Will they not both fall into a pit?
LUKE 6:39

FAITH, HOPE, AND love are meant to characterize every Christian life, and all who have been baptized, and have not through their own fault destroyed the life of the Holy Spirit within them, possess these virtues to one degree or another. But different people possess them in different measures. For one person, faith will come relatively easily, while hope will be difficult to maintain. For another, faith and hope are less problematic, but love comes only with a struggle. Another will love with a certain ease, but will find faith constantly weak and under attack. It has been noted that a person's main struggles in life will often surround one of these three virtues. Identifying which can give us insight into our spiritual lives.

It is good to have a healthy self-understanding concerning faith, hope, and love. What follows is a brief self-assessment tool to further our self-knowledge in the light of these virtues. We can then know better what strengths we bring to our leadership and where we need to look for others to complement our leadership. While Christian conviction is not susceptible of being measured exactly, there are questions that can help us to assess the depth and strength of our conviction, and where we need to grow.

FAITH: SEEING THE UNSEEN TRULY

- Do I have a quick and consistent sense for the invisible world, for the existence and presence of God, and for the realities behind material things? *or* Do I easily get distracted from the most important unseen things by immediately seen ones?

- Does my knowledge of the truths of the faith—God as provident, loving and active, the human race as fallen but graced, the work of Christ as the one hope for the world—affect and integrate the way I see the world and act in it? *or* Do such truths sit on the surface of my mind without much practical effect on how I think and behave?

- Am I able to see in those I meet the image of Christ whatever their outward appearance? *or* Do I tend to evaluate people and events around me according to a this-worldly judgment? Am I easily influenced by a person's wealth, or position, or beauty of form and face?

- Do I consistently apply Christian principles in evaluating events passing before me? *or* Do I tend to slide into the categories of success used by this world rather than by Christ?

- Do I have the strength of mind to hold to my Christian convictions where they are contrary to the currents around me? *or* Am I easily influenced by others who don't have faith, such that I begin to take on their way of thinking and acting?

◈   Do the realities of the invisible world, God, the angels, our immortal souls, color my thinking and behavior as I go through
the day? *or* Is it a great weight upon me not to be in agreement
with what seems the "normal" way of looking at things?

◈   Do I hold my possessions with a certain lightness and detach-
ment under the clear conviction that they are quickly passing
and of little worth? *or* Do I tend to being greedy, to storing
things up, to calculating my earthly prosperity, to aiming at security, to delighting in being wealthy and having nice things?

HOPE: ORIENTING MYSELF TO A FUTURE GOOD

◈   Am I resilient in the face of setbacks and sufferings? *or* Do I find
myself easily discouraged by opposition or failure, or tempted
to give up what I have been doing?

◈   Do I firmly grasp the truth that God is in the process of working his saving will in human history and that all will one day be
well? *or* Do I have a difficult time remembering or believing the
plan of salvation for the world and for myself?

◈   Does joy have a significant place in my life? *or* Do I tend to a
gloomy outlook on things, to see the worst of possible scenarios
before me?

◈   Is my life characterized by a fundamental serenity? *or* Am I constantly anxious and nervous about the state of the world, or of
the Church, or of my country, or of my life?

- Am I able to live in a generally temperate way? *or* Do I find it difficult to put off gratification or fulfillment in the present for the sake of a future good? Do I find myself using food or drink or comfort or pleasure as a way of "medicating" my inner desolation?

- Do I remain hopeful in the face of my own or others' suffering? *or* Do I avert my eyes from suffering because I find it too desolating to deal with?

- Do I desire and preserve times and places of silence, contemplation, and recollection? *or* Do I fill my hours with the distractions of electronic media: music, news, TV, information? Do I have a tendency to become a media junkie?

LOVE: LIVING FOR GOD AND OTHERS RATHER THAN FOR SELF

- Is it easy for me to be involved in the projects and plans and concerns of others? *or* Do I find it difficult to motivate myself in matters that don't immediately touch on my interests?

- Is the main concern of my leadership the coming of Christ's kingdom? *or* Do I pay great attention to how my leadership or my performance is judged by others? Does praise make me soar and criticism make me sour?

- Do I delight in the good fortune, talents, and accomplishments of others? *or* Do I tend to be envious of others' accomplishments and praise, and jealous of their gifts and the attention they are being paid? Do I find myself disliking certain people for no reason except that they are very good at something?

◈ Can I handle personal insult with equanimity? *or* Am I easily offended when people don't pay me the respect I think I deserve?

◈ Do I pursue the spirit of the law rather than its letter? *or* Do I tend to be legalistic, to pride myself on doing things the right way? Do I get easily irritated by people who are not "following the rules"?

◈ Do I forgive easily and from the heart? *or* Do I tend to carry grudges, to remember and count up offenses against me?

◈ Do I find my deepest delight in being a son or daughter of God, content to let him arrange affairs as he sees fit? *or* Do I find myself bargaining with God, totaling up the things I have done for him or given up in his service, so as to hold him accountable and to demand something in return?

TRUE LEADERSHIP

— NOTES —

CHAPTER 6

THE SECOND FOUNDATION OF TRUE LEADERSHIP: CHARACTER

"Who Am I?"

I look to a day when people will not be judged by the color of their skin, but by the content of their character.

MARTIN LUTHER KING

Put off your old nature which belongs to your former manner of life and is corrupt through deceitful lusts, and be renewed in the spirit of your minds, and put on the new nature, created after the likeness of God in true righteousness and holiness.

EPHESIANS 4:22–24

IF THE FIRST requisite of true leadership is Christian conviction, the second is Christian character.

Most of us have a general sense of what character means in a leadership context. Someone of good character will have certain traits, such as truthfulness, self-control, maturity, responsibility, and industriousness. This is true as far as it goes, but it doesn't go quite far enough. We will want to pursue this with more clarity, and ask what it means to gain a Christian character.

GAINING THE CHARACTER OF CHRIST

The beginning of the letter to the Hebrews gives a description of Christ that includes this phrase: "He reflects the glory of God and bears the very stamp of his nature, upholding the universe by his word of power" (Heb 1:3). Jesus bears the "stamp" of God's nature: the word used in Greek for this is "character." In another passage describing Christ, Paul says that "he is the image of the invisible God" (Col 1:15): the word used in Greek for this is "icon." These scriptural words, image and stamp, give us a clue as to what Christians mean when they speak of Christian character.

To bear a character is to be formed into a particular image. As a coin is stamped into an enduring form, so we are molded into the form of the one we are following. We share in the nature of the one in whose image we are made. This is why there can be no such thing as a self-generated character. We are all in search of an identity; in search of someone to "identify" with. The question is: who is that someone? Whose image will I bear?

When God brought us into being, he created us "in his image and likeness" (Gen 1:26–27). He made us to bear his stamp, to share in some mysterious way in his own nature. This is why we dare to call God our Father: children have the same nature as their parents. Stars and planets, flowers and trees, birds and cattle, all were created by God, but none can call him Father; none of them were made in his image; none of them were created to bear his stamp, his character. This is the incomprehensibly high destiny given to humans.

Jesus elucidates this truth in a noteworthy encounter with the Pharisees. Here is St. Matthew's account of that meeting:

> Then the Pharisees went and took counsel how to entangle him in his talk. And they sent their disciples to him, along with the Herodians, saying, "Teacher, we know that you are true, and teach the way of God truthfully, and care for no man; for you do not regard the position of men. Tell us, then, what you think. Is it lawful to pay taxes to

Caesar, or not?" But Jesus, aware of their malice, said, "Why put me to the test, you hypocrites? Show me the money for the tax." And they brought him a coin. And Jesus said to them, "Whose likeness and inscription is this?" They said, "Caesar's." Then he said to them, "Render therefore to Caesar the things that are Caesar's, and to God the things that are God's." When they heard it, they marveled; and they left him and went away. (Mt 22:15–22)

"Whose likeness [icon] is this?" Jesus wants to know whose image the coin bears, because that will make clear to whom it belongs. The coin is stamped with Caesar's image; it therefore belongs to Caesar. But the human bears the stamp, the image or character, of God, and therefore belongs to God. In this encounter Jesus is not cleverly dodging a difficult question: he is calling the Pharisees to their true allegiance.

Humans, oddly enough, are not yet fully created. We have not yet reached our final form. God confers upon us a remarkable dignity by allowing us to participate in bringing our own creation to its final end. It is as if a sculptor had worked a statue to a certain point of completion and then had breathed life into it and asked its cooperation in helping to apply the finishing touches. But though created to bear God's imprint, we have the freedom to reject our created purpose and to attempt to impose a different image upon ourselves. The operation never works; it only distorts and ultimately destroys the true image given us. This was the sin of our first parents, and has been the sad tale of the human race ever since. The narrow way that leads to life is not just a matter of following a set of rules: it is the process by which we are changed, away from whatever idolatrous images we have been attempting to stamp upon ourselves, into the image of God in Christ.

THE HEART OF THE MATTER

The word most often used in the Scripture to refer to our essential inner being, where we are most truly ourselves and where our character is stamped, is the word "heart." We have come to think of the heart mainly as the seat of the emotions. But the Scripture uses the word in a wider and more profound sense, to include mind, will, affections, the whole of us. We are to love God with our whole heart, with everything we are, from the depth of our being.

When God sent the prophet Samuel to anoint a king of Israel, he said to him, "the Lord sees not as man sees; man looks on the outward appearance, but the Lord looks on the heart," meaning by this the inner person (1 Sam 16:7). Jesus uses the word this way when he says, "The good man out of the good treasure of his heart produces good, and the evil man out of his evil treasure produces evil; for out of the abundance of the heart his mouth speaks" (Lk 6:45). "The heart is deceitful above all things, and desperately corrupt," says the prophet Jeremiah of fallen human nature (Jer 17:9). Jesus was grieved and angered by the "hardness of heart" of some who heard him (Mk 3:5); and he tells us that it is the "pure of heart" who will see God (Mt 5:8). To gain a Christian character means to be changed in heart, to participate with the action of God as he renews and completes the work of creation he has begun in us. It means to "put on Christ" such that we take on ever more truly the image of God as shown us in his Son. To follow Christ is to "become" Christ, to bear his image. "It is no longer I who live, but Christ who lives in me" (Gal 2:20). Forging a Christian character is not possible without the action of God. We have our necessary part to play, but we cannot regain the image of Christ unless we are made new by God's free gift.

CHARACTER AND LEADERSHIP

It was noted earlier that true leadership is not mainly what someone does, but who that person is. This statement becomes clearer as we understand the importance of character in leadership. Our leadership comes not from

The Second Foundation: Character

us, but from the one whose image we bear, whose nature we are taking on. Paul referred to this truth when he said to those he was leading, "Be imitators of me as I am of Christ" (1 Cor 11:1). He didn't mean that the Christians in Corinth should take on his mannerisms or quirks, or try to walk with the same gait or develop the same laugh. He was talking about his character, the life of Christ within him. The true leader is imitating Christ, not in a superficial way, but by putting on a new nature and forging a new heart. Whatever leadership role we have taken on, if it is not rooted in our character, and if we are not calling those we are leading to imitate us as we are imitating Christ, our leadership will be lacking.

No one appreciates a hypocrite. But it is difficult to avoid becoming hypocrites unless we embrace as a daily task the habit of molding our character to that of Christ. Positions of leadership and responsibility bring with them trials, pressures, and temptations; and the greater the responsibility, the greater the temptations. Abraham Lincoln once said, "Nearly all men can stand adversity, but if you want to test a man's character, give him power." Those who lead require strong character—virtue—in order to fulfill their responsibilities without losing their balance. We all know examples of talented people whose leadership was overthrown by their lack of character. They may have had any number of impressive qualities that gained them influence, but they were also dishonest, or lazy, or drank too much, or let their sexual desires run rampant, or sought power selfishly. Such people lead others down destructive paths, and often pull their world down upon their own heads. Developing self-mastery over the various powers that we've been given—of mind, of body, of emotion, of personality, of wealth, of natural gift, of education—all under the guidance of the Holy Spirit, is essential for true leadership.

There are many good resources that deal with character development: how to be properly humble, courageous, honest, and generous. By and large we know what these virtues are. The hard thing is not so much to identify what makes for good character, but rather to grow in character, and that requires time and persevering effort. There is no short-cut to strong character. Virtue grows only by practice.

Once the nature of Christian character is seen, those who aspire to true leadership can avoid two common temptations concerning character in leadership.

The first is the temptation to pursue self-improvement for its own sake. Certain character qualities are so evidently good, so clearly esteemed by others, that we can desire them for the wrong reasons. We can seek a particular virtue, not for the sake of its intrinsic goodness, but to serve ourselves, to think well of ourselves, and to hold our heads up above others who do not possess it. Pride is often used to conquer lesser vices. Someone who has remarkable self-control, or who works with extraordinary energy, or who runs dangerous personal risks in pursuit of a goal, is admired and praised by others, and this can become a sufficient motive for attempting to gain the virtue in question. There is also, more subtly, our own self-regard in play. No one likes the degrading experience of being enslaved to lower passions. It is humiliating to be the plaything of desires for food and drink or sexual stimulation, or to be paralyzed by cowardice. Those who have a high code of honor may consider it beneath themselves to lie or flatter or act in a way that would put a stain upon their sense of self-respect. Virtue, when not received as a gift from God and oriented to others, tends to pride and self-conceit. We can strive for strength of character, not to please another, but to please ourselves. This is not the way to gain the character of Christ, whose entire being was oriented to doing his Father's will.

A second temptation is what might be called the utilitarian desire for good character. Because behaving in certain ways "works," because it is more effective for getting things done, those who aspire to positions of leadership and who hope for success will aim at gaining those character qualities as a matter of practical utility. The phrase "honesty is the best policy" is an example of this attitude. Because honesty, in most cases and in the long run, tends to get better results than lying and deception, the one who wants to be successful is advised to be honest. The problem is that while honesty is usually the best policy, it is not always; some have become wealthy and powerful and have died in their beds pursuing a policy of trickery and falsehood. Those who take this utilitarian attitude are not interested in forging within themselves the image of Christ. They rather orient their pursuit of character to a calculated scheme, reckoning up what will get them ahead. They will be industrious, or self-controlled in speech, or prudent, not because they are filling out in themselves their true form under the guiding influence of the Holy Spirit, but because they know that such habits will give them the power or position they desire. If it seems clear in a given instance that honesty, or justice, or straight dealing, or temperate behavior, or loyalty, is not likely to get them what they want, they will have no problem in making an exception. They call this worldly wisdom, understanding the way things really are. They will say that it is impossible to get on in life if one is too rigid about such matters. They will pay a lot of attention to their public image, and will be happy to seem more virtuous than they are.

Those who aim at true leadership, who pursue virtue in order to lose themselves, whose goal is to put aside self-interest and embrace the image of Christ, will not think about character in this utilitarian way. They will attempt to act honestly because Christ is the truth, and honesty an aspect of his character, and they will not worry about whether their honesty gets them ahead or gets them into trouble. They will practice courage because Christ is courageous, not because it wins them admiration. They will struggle for self-control because they know they are called to it as belonging to Christ, not because it will increase their ability to get ahead. Recognizing Christ's humility, they will avoid being showy and making a display of themselves, and they will often try to hide the good points of their character from others. They know that as they share Christ's character, they will share his position and his fate in this world. "You will be hated by all for my name's sake" (Mt 10:22). Such is the expectation Jesus gives to those who follow him, who bear his image.

THE PROBLEM OF PROCEDURAL LEADERSHIP

There is currently a tendency to downplay or give mere lip-service to conviction and character, these two essential qualities of the good leader. Because they are costly, and require time and effort to acquire, many avoid dealing with them, and look for a shorter and easier road to leadership. What comes of this attitude is a great plague of our time, what might be called "procedural" leadership. True leadership begins by examining what is good and wise for all concerned, and then leads with conviction into that truth and goodness, taking personal responsibility for decisions made along the way. Those who engage in procedural leadership do more than simply establish proper procedures in the institutions they are leading, an important aspect of competent leadership. They go further, and attempt to reduce everything to sets of rules that require no special quality of mind or will to implement, and that leave those in responsibility free from the need to invest themselves in what they are leading. As long as the proper protocols are followed, deeper questions are not raised, such as: Is this the right or wrong thing to do? Will this aid or hinder the good? What will be the effect of this upon various individuals and on the society as a whole? What is the just or courageous way of proceeding? At the root of procedural leadership is often cowardice: reluctance to take a stand, unwillingness to make a judgment and be called to account for it, or fear of facing the opposition that true leadership inevitably provokes. Such leadership by procedure becomes defensive; it produces endless coils of time-consuming bureaucracy; it results in mediocrity and stagnation in the institutions it has infected; it suffocates those under it; it inhibits creative initiative. And all the time those who "lead" in such a manner can say, "I have followed all the procedures and carefully noted all the protocols." Institutions, groups, associations, agencies, or businesses that are led in this way will become inhuman places, and will eventually grow sickly and founder unless they are kept alive through artificial means.

The Second Foundation: Character

Clarity of conviction and strength of character are more important in leadership than any talent or gift or skill or technical training a person may possess. They are the necessary foundation for any adequate leadership, and nothing can take their place. Any discussion of leadership that bypasses them is not addressing the most important leadership questions.

— NOTES —

~   CHAPTER 7   ~

ASSESSING CHRISTIAN CHARACTER

If anyone loves righteousness, wisdom's labors are virtues; for she teaches self-control and prudence, justice and courage; nothing in life is more profitable for men than these.

WISDOM 8:7

THE CARDINAL VIRTUES AND CHARACTER

We have looked at the theological virtues as those strengths of our inner being given us through grace that make possible the restoration of the image of Christ in us. The cardinal, or human, virtues, given us at our creation, are available to everyone. They are enhanced and brought to their true form by the presence of the Holy Spirit as he fills out the image of Christ within us.

The Catechism of the Catholic Church describes the cardinal virtues this way: "Human virtues are firm attitudes, stable dispositions, habitual perfections of intellect and will that govern our actions, order our passions, and guide our conduct according to reason and faith. They make possible ease, self-mastery, and joy in leading a morally good life" (§1804). There are many excellent treatments of the virtues. Here we only want to briefly describe them and to note their importance in true leadership. The cardinal virtues are four, and are ordered according to an understanding of our anthropology, our human nature. The first is prudence, practical wisdom, the virtue that allows us to perceive, in the midst of the complexities of life, what way of acting will most conduce to goodness, and to act according to that perception. The second, justice, is the virtue by which we give to each person, including God, his or her due. These are the highest natural virtues; to be fully prudent and fully just is to come to natural human perfection. The second pair of virtues, courage and temperance, give us mastery over ourselves such that we can act prudently and justly. Courage enables us to overcome serious difficulties in pursuing what is good and true; temperance keeps us from falling prey to an excessive desire for pleasure, thereby giving us the freedom to pursue truth and goodness.

The virtues, theological and cardinal, are the pattern of the life of God within us. To say that we are growing in virtue leading to strength of character is another way of saying we are growing in holiness and regaining the image of Christ.

As with the theological virtues, we have prepared a brief assessment tool for the cardinal virtues. The point is to better understand where our character is strong and where it is weak or in need of support. Understanding this will help us as we lead; it will deepen our understanding of ourselves, and point us toward making up our lacks, by giving special attention to those areas where we are weakest, and by relying on others for help in leadership.

These virtues grow in us by the help of God and by our own practice. If we want to grow in virtue, both prayer and practice are called for.

Prudence (Practical Wisdom)

Prudence, despite its somewhat boring associations, is a majestic virtue. It is not a stance of being safe and overly careful; it is rather the princely habit of choosing what is good, in accordance with reason and truth, in the midst of the business of life. It can be prudent to exercise care; it can be prudent to do something bold and risky. The question at issue is: what will best secure the good in this situation?

Prudence is not a technique, and can only be gained over time in the crucible of life's experience. Because of this, to be young is, at least to some degree, to be imprudent. The Wisdom literature in the Scriptures contains an immense endowment of prudential wisdom. A consistent diet of those books can help forge the prudent character.

Prudence is sometimes called the "form" of the other human virtues. This means that unless an act is prudent, unless it tends to the good according to reason and truth, it cannot be virtuous at all. We cannot be courageous unless the act of courage corresponds to reality. We cannot be temperate unless that temperance is guided by what is good and real, by right reason, by prudence.

- Do I regularly finish what I set out to do? *or* Do I find myself getting excited about an idea or project, but then lose steam, and stop before I have completed it?

- Do I willingly seek advice from others? *or* Am I irritated when advice is proffered to me?

- Do I approach a task or a project with a mind open to creative non-compromising alternatives? *or* Do I tend to be stubborn and immovable about my way of doing things?

- Am I usually well-prepared for the task at hand? *or* Do I find myself regularly flat-footed and "shooting from the hip"?

- Do I make room in my exercise of leadership for the gifts of others? *or* Do I tend to be over-controlling and micro-managing?

+ Am I able to distinguish important from unimportant issues? *or* Do I spend too much time on minor matters and leave major ones unattended?

+ Is my leadership characterized by calmness and steadiness? *or* Am I regularly paralyzed by excessive fretfulness and anxiety?

+ Is my primary concern in leadership for the people I am leading? *or* Do I tend to concern myself with things rather than persons?

+ Do I speak carefully and within my knowledge about questions at hand? *or* Am I quick to give my opinion on things I know little about?

+ Do I deal with those around me in a straightforward and honest manner? *or* Am I willing to use flattery and cajolery to manipulate situations in my favor?

+ Am I willing to suffer setbacks in my projects in order to safeguard fundamental principles? *or* Am I willing to "bend the rules" in order to achieve my goals?

Justice

Justice it the habitual practice of giving to each person what is his or her due, in the light of what is true, with the common good in mind.

Unlike prudence, which comes only with long experience, the sense of justice is strong in us from the time we are very young. Even little children have a keen sense of what is just. "That's not fair!" comes out of young mouths frequently. But while we are touchy about injustice done to us, we tend to be less ready to see the injustice we do to others.

Justice, in this like all the virtues, is founded on what is true; it helps us to adjust our inner being and our behavior to what is real. When truths about who God is and who we are as his creatures fall by the wayside, justice becomes a very slippery concept. Why should a government not do away with whole portions of the society for the sake of pursuing a social project? Because to do so would be unjust: it would be to take from others what we have no right to take, namely their lives. But, as the Russian novelist Dostoevsky famously noted, without God, everything is permitted. If we are not creatures of the Divine Being who have been accorded an inviolable dignity coming from him, if we are accidentally existing conglomerations of dancing molecules, there is no compelling reason why we shouldn't be liquidated at the convenience of someone or something else. No truth, no justice.

The unwillingness of many in our society to make truth claims has given rise in our time to an emotive orientation to justice: that is just which I feel to be just, and that is unjust which offends me. One sees this disfiguration of justice in most of the disputed issues of the day. Questions concerning the taking of life, of abortion and euthanasia and embryonic stem cell research, are properly questions of justice, of what is due and what is not due to the various people involved. Questions concerning marriage, whether about divorce laws, or same-sex unions, or child support issues, are questions of justice, of what is owed to whom by whom, and how such matters affect the common good. Nonetheless, one finds that much, even most of the discussion around such questions has little to do with objective principles of justice. We are rather given a stream of personal stories that are meant to produce an emotional response, and objective principles of justice fall by the wayside. Because emotional responses are so easily manipulated, such emotivism tends ultimately to result in serious injustice. As the writer Flannery O'Connor pungently put it, there is a tenderness that can lead to the gas chambers.

The same attitude can be found in the current prevalence of the tyranny of the offended. Let someone say that a given action or policy or statement offended him or her, and all are supposed to stop in their tracks and abjectly apologize to the one offended, whatever the offense may be. The criterion for determining such an offense is simply what the person felt about it. But such matters have little to do with personal feeling. It is indeed wrong to give offense; but to give offense means to act unjustly, to have withheld the respect due to another. Those who are offended need to have objectively just grounds for feeling offended. If such grounds are not present, then they need to practice justice themselves by adjusting their inner response to what is objectively true, lest they become unjust in their grievance. No truth, no justice.

* Do I attempt consistently to give to God what is his due, whether it be worship or obedience or gratitude? *or* Do I allow my orientation to God be determined by how I am currently feeling, or by personal preference rather than principle?

* Do I make moral judgments according to principles of objective right and wrong? *or* Are my moral judgments based on sentiment and feeling?

* Is my natural inclination to be slow to accuse and to believe accusations against others? *or* Am I ready to accuse, and quick to believe accusations?

* Am I quick to accuse myself and defend others? *or* Am I, rather, quick to defend myself and to criticize others?

* Do I carefully protect the good name of others and resist speaking against them? *or* Am I given to gossip, to tale bearing, to detraction, to speaking behind others' backs?

* Do I accept criticism from others in a reasonable spirit, looking

for what is true in it? *or* Am I easily offended or outraged by others' criticism of me?

* Do I tend to appeal to principle and reason to influence people? *or* Do I depend on flattery or fear or emotional manipulation to get my way?

* When in a situation of conflict, do I deal with people fairly, giving due recognition to their arguments or their positions even while disagreeing with them? *or* Do I exaggerate my claims and diminish theirs, and insist on absolute victory?

* Do I attempt to see things from another's point of view? *or* Do I think that anyone who sees things differently from me has no grounds for their position?

* Do I have a disciplined sensitivity to human suffering? *or* Do I find myself either insensitive and unaware of the suffering and plight of others, or mawkish and overwhelmed by it?

* Am I careful to respect the possessions of others, whether of material goods or relationships or position or reputation? *or* Do I tend to take what will be of advantage to me without thinking of the consequences for another?

* Do I handle those I meet with a certain equality of dignity? *or* Am I obsequious toward superiors and toward the popular, wealthy and powerful, and autocratic toward those under me, and the weak and unpopular?

* Am I even-handed in dealing with those I have responsibility for? *or* Do I play favorites with subordinates?

+ Am I attentive to what will serve the common good? *or* Do I think of my own or another's individual interests first, with little regard for the common welfare?

+ Am I even-handed in my perception and practice of justice? *or* Do I tend to excuse the injustices of certain people and institutions because of my loyalty to them, while condemning others because I dislike them?

Courage

Courage is the habit of conquering difficult obstacles in achieving what is good. It involves the readiness to suffer for a good cause.

Courage is not fearlessness. Where there is no fear, there is no need for courage. Fear is not necessarily bad, nor irrational. We are meant to fear those things that will destroy us. Fear helps us stay alive and healthy. But we can fall prey to irrational fears that need to be overcome. Or we fear reasonably enough, but for the sake of a greater good we may need to put aside our fear, as does the soldier who sensibly fears what will physically harm or kill him, yet conquers his fear to defend his home and family.

Paradoxically, the way to gain courage, the means of conquering fear, is by fearing rightly. Jesus tells his followers that they should have no anxiety about anything; the Psalms are full of expressions of confidence and courage in the face of enemies and dangers. If we ask what the foundation this courage is built upon, the answer is the proper fear of God. "I tell you, my friends, do not fear those who kill the body, and after that have no more that they can do. But I will warn you whom to fear: fear him who, after he has killed, has power to cast into hell; yes, I tell you, fear him!" (Lk 12:4–5). Rightly understanding who God is and who we are in relation to him, rightly both trusting and fearing him, sets us free from fears of a lesser kind.

True leadership demands courage, because those who lead will find themselves called regularly to suffer. Paul gives a poignant catalogue of such suffering in his second letter to the Corinthians.

> Are they servants of Christ? I am a better one—I am talking like a madman—with far greater labors, far more imprisonments, with countless beatings, and often near death. Five times I have received at the hands of the Jews the forty lashes less one. Three times I have been beaten with rods; once I was stoned. Three times I have been shipwrecked; a night and a day I have been adrift at sea; on frequent journeys, in danger from rivers, danger from robbers, danger from my own people, danger from Gentiles, danger in the city, danger in the wilderness, danger at sea, danger from false brethren; in toil and hardship, through many a sleepless night, in hunger and thirst, often without food, in cold and exposure. And, apart from other things, there is the daily pressure upon me of my anxiety for all the churches. Who is weak, and I am not weak? Who is made to fall, and I am not indignant? (2 Cor 11:23–29)

Responsibility always brings hardship of one sort or another.

- Do I face necessary conflict with steadiness? *or* Do I tend to avoid conflict due to fear?

- Do I say what needs to be said even if I am not sure of its reception? *or* Do I find myself not saying things I should because I fear rejection or ridicule?

- Do I face falsehood and injustice squarely and confidently? *or* Do I emphasize tolerance and getting along even when there is an issue of truth or justice at stake?

- Am I willing to assume responsibility for the decisions I make? *or* Do I try to slough blame off on others, or claim that I was only following protocols?

- Do I lead from a positive forward vision, recognizing but not being overwhelmed by challenges? *or* Is my leadership largely reactive, based on calculating minimal risk and avoiding suffering?

- Do I struggle on through defeat and setback? *or* Do I easily get discouraged and give up? In my discouragement do I find myself resentful, bitter, and indifferent to people and institutions?

- Do I persevere in a project even if the excitement has worn off? Am I willing to stick to the mundane and routine details of life? Do I finish the job? *or* Do I stop when I encounter tedium or boredom or lack of recognition in my task?

- Am I able to make important decisions with a certain confidence and ease? *or* Do I get paralyzed in the face of significant decisions, fearing commitment and the limitation of choices?

- Do I pursue reasonable options before determining a course of action? *or* Am I drawn to impulsive decisions and risky situations that might put myself or others in danger or lead to needless difficulties?

- Do I fear offending God? *or* Do I fear offending other people?

Temperance

Temperance is the habitual mastery of our life-giving and life-sustaining powers according to the order of reason and for the sake of love. God in his goodness has made the activities of creating and maintaining life pleasurable and meaningful. He need not have; but in God's plan, our duties and our pleasures were meant to coincide. Temperance preserves our inner order such that we do not turn inward and selfishly indulge ourselves in the pursuit of pleasure. It protects wisdom and justice. The intemperate person cannot be wise, and cannot be just. Habitual intemperance blinds and enslaves; habitual temperance opens our eyes and sets us free.

It is true that temperance does not address our highest faculties, and that therefore failings in temperance are not the most serious of sins. Yet it is also true that, practically speaking, temperance is of great importance. Temperance is like the roof of a house. No one would say that the roof is the most significant part of a home; that honor might go to the family room, or the kitchen, or the master bedroom. But if the roof is badly damaged, the whole house will soon become unlivable. This is why so much emphasis has traditionally been placed on gaining the virtue of temperance. The leader who is intemperate in eating or drinking or sexual matters will be seriously hampered in other matters of the highest importance.

- Do I make decisions on the basis of what is reasonable or according to principle? Am I willing to forego comfort without complaint in the service of love or truth? *or* Do I tend toward what will keep me most comfortable, and carefully avoid situations that will bring discomfort?

- Am I moderate in my habits? *or* Do I tend to overdo things (eating, drinking, sleeping, working, arguing)? Do I have a hard time knowing when to stop? What is the state of my "internal barometer"?

- Is my sexual behavior appropriate to my state of life, and my sexual desires rightly moderated? *or* Am I at the mercy of my desires and unable to master myself sexually?

* Do I think and speak with moderation? *or* Do I tend to push my views to extremes?

* Am I true to my word, and faithful in fulfilling commitments? *or* Do I tend to say yes to everything, but fail to do anything well? Do I find myself regularly overbooking?

* Is my media intake ordered and restrained? *or* Do I need to be "plugged in" all the time? Am I a technology junkie? Do I have regular difficulty with internet pornography? Am I constantly reading blogs and news stories? Do I spend too much time with video games, or social media, email, and texting? Do I take telephone calls or engage in texting when I am in face-to-face conversations?

DISCOURAGEMENT, OR THE UPWARD CALL

It can be daunting to look at a list of virtues and a description of virtuous behavior. An honest person can find something for self-criticism in almost every item on the list. But the point of laying out the virtues is not to be crushed by them; it is to see the overall form of the true human, and to cooperate with the work of the Holy Spirit as he leads us into the character of Christ. The true leader is not perfect in every virtue. But the true leader sees the importance of growing in virtue, and understands that gaining virtue is a combination of grace first, along with effort and time.

— NOTES —

CHAPTER 8

THE THIRD FOUNDATION OF TRUE LEADERSHIP: VOCATION

"What Is God Requiring of Me?"

> *God has created me to do him some definite service. He has committed some work to me which he has not committed to another. I have my mission. I may never know it in this life, but I shall be told it in the next. I am a link in a chain, a bond of connection between persons. He has not created me for naught. I shall do good; I shall do His work.*
>
> JOHN HENRY NEWMAN

> *I therefore, a prisoner for the Lord, beg you to lead a life worthy of the calling to which you have been called, with all lowliness and meekness, with patience, forbearing one another in love.*
>
> EPHESIANS 4:1–2

WE HAVE LOOKED at conviction and character, the first two foundations of true leadership. We are now ready to examine the other three: vocation, gifts, and skills. Putting these third, fourth, and fifth is not a way of saying that they are unimportant. Quite the contrary: they are crucial aspects of leadership.

WHAT IS VOCATION?

The origin of the word vocation is the Latin verb *vocare*, "to call." This origin gives an important clue as to the meaning of the word. If a person has a calling, it means that there is someone else who is doing the calling. We are responding to another. It makes no sense to "call" ourselves. Discerning and responding to a vocation means first that we have been created by God with an important purpose in mind, different for each of us, and therefore needs to be listened for. One of life's important tasks is to learn to listen to what God has in mind for us, to keep our ears open to that which we are called to be and do.

In the language of the Church, vocation has often referred to the call to priestly or religious life. Used this way, the phrase "to have a vocation" means to understand that God is intending a life of consecrated celibacy. The call to consecration can indeed be a call into a particularly intensive form of leadership. The Holy Father, bishops, priests, members of religious orders, exercise significant leadership. All who live as consecrated celibates have a special call, whether individually or by their common life and witness, to influence the world toward the Kingdom of God. This places a unique burden of leadership upon them.

Vocation, though, means more than the call to consecrated celibacy. All Christians have a vocation, a set of tasks and relationships, a stance of life prepared for them by God and needing their cooperation, that will bring into play their energies and gifts, and will be the place of their own continuing transformation. The Church speaks this way about the vocation of marriage and family, or of a vocation to a particular kind of work or of service that will make a unique contribution to his work in the world.

.
.
.

SETTING THE PROPER CONTEXT
FOR DISCERNING VOCATION

Because our vocation comes from another, from God himself, the soil in which our vocation grows is prayer, a living relationship with the one who is issuing the call. During his visit to the United States, Pope Benedict XVI spoke of the primacy of prayer in vocational discernment. "Prayer... is the first means by which we come to know the Lord's will for our lives. To the extent that we teach young people to pray, and to pray well, we will be cooperating with God's call. Programs, plans and projects have their place; but the discernment of a vocation is above all the fruit of an intimate dialogue between the Lord and his disciples. Young people, if they know how to pray, can be trusted to know what to do with God's call." Prayer comes first.

Discerning a vocation eventually involves sorting out specific practical questions. But before we are ready to ask those specific questions, we will need to place them in their proper context. Until we do, our vocational discernment will be fraught with perplexity and disappointment. To set this context, we might pose three questions.

The First Question: Why am I here?
In the midst of life's necessary duties and occupations, these central questions come upon everyone: "What am I doing here? What is the point of my life? What gives it meaning?" This is more than just idle philosophical speculation. The answer has a practical bearing on all we do. We know, if sometimes only dimly, that our existence is not accidental or arbitrary, that we were created for a purpose, and that our happiness is tied up with finding what that purpose is. However much we try to distract ourselves, these questions will keep coming up and will gnaw at us, often at the most unlikely times: Am I fulfilling my true purpose? Am I living meaningfully, or am I half-alive, missing the adventure I was called to or sleeping

through it? We fear, deep within us, the real and tragic possibility that we might entirely miss the point of our lives.

Because everyone faces these questions, there is a constant litany of answers on offer. Here are a few of them:

- I am here to be successful, to look out for Number One.

- I am here to have a good career and to leave a legacy behind.

- I am here to experience life to the fullest.

- I am here to construct an interesting and meaningful lifestyle.

- I am here to find my soul-mate.

- I am here to make a difference, to make the world a better place.

- I am here to work for the coming of the Kingdom of Christ.

Here is the answer Jesus gave to this question: "You shall love the Lord your God with all your heart, and with all your soul, and with all your mind. This is the great and first commandment. And a second is like it. You shall love your neighbor as yourself. On these two commandments depend all the law and the prophets" (Mt 22:37–40).

Why are we here? The simple and sufficient answer is: We are here to learn to love; to overcome the pride and selfishness that are endemic to us as fallen creatures, and to be filled with the new divine life that comes from God. We are here to learn self-forgetfulness and to become worthy to inherit the kingdom that can only be gained by those who love. We are called, each of us, to become great lovers.

We need to be crystal clear on this point, because it provides the basis for every true vocation. All vocations, whether those that give shape to the whole of our lives, or those that are more limited in scope, are roads by which we respond to this fundamental call. Charity, love, is the purpose of our existence, the point of it all. If we are being transformed in love, we are fulfilling our purpose even in the midst of profound suffering and difficulty. If we are not learning to love, no matter what else we may be accomplishing, we are wasting our time and missing our lives.

FALSE IMAGES OF THE SUCCESSFUL LIFE. It may seem obvious to say that God calls us to love. Who doubts that this is at the heart of the Christian faith? The word love is so overused as to become irritating. But the implications of this truth are not always clear, particularly in the area of vocation.

We carry in our minds, sometimes only half-consciously, an image of what it means to be a successful person, one that emerges when the inner experience of who we are comes into contact with the many images that surround us. We are bombarded from all sides by such images. They come from our families, from the prevalent attitudes of the society in which we live, from our education, from the incessant presentation of attractive and successful people through books and electronic media, from friendships and in conversations with others. Faced with these many images, we then construct an ideal picture of success, a framework of what our lives should look like, whether in family life, or education and career, or social life, or service to God. In the light of that ideal picture, we evaluate our current circumstances. If we think we are more or less attaining to our image of success, we feel confident and comfortable. If our life makes a poor showing against it, we grow despondent and listless. If we are attaining success according to our chosen image and it is not bringing us a sense of meaning, we go into crisis. All of this is a natural, even a necessary, process. We are not yet fully formed, and we need help from outside ourselves to grow into our true shape.

Our problem arises when our image of success is not founded on the image of God, Christ, who is the exemplar of the true and normal human life. We often construct an alloyed image: we join Christ to the categories of this-worldly success, merging genuine excellences of life and character with much that is passing and has little to do with God's work in us. The supposedly successful Christian has a strong faith, along with good health, plenty of money, adorable and happy children, a stress-free marriage, a meaningful job, and good looks into the bargain. We don't ignore Christ; but we don't seek his mind alone in fashioning the picture of our life from the ground up. We do not use his calculus for measuring our success. To the degree that our thoughts are not God's thoughts in this matter, we can find ourselves angry or discouraged about his manner of dealing with us.

If we are still sorting out the basic decisions that will set our future course, we can sometimes expect God simply to tell us what to do. We are ready to obey: just send the letter or text and we'll be off and running. We may find that our vocational discernment is not easily resolving itself. We try one path and it seems to lead nowhere; we try another and a door unexpectedly closes on us; we experiment with a third and we find it doesn't suit us. We have a hard time sifting our own deepest desires. We feel as though we can't really begin living until this matter

of marriage or celibacy, this question of what career to pursue or what job to take, this issue of whether to marry this particular person or not, sorts itself out. We feel as though we are "on hold," unable to engage our real life. In the midst of this, heaven seems silent, not speaking with a clear voice and not giving us what we need to get on with our lives. We can grow impatient and frustrated. We think that either God is not being fair with us, or that there is something wrong with us and our ability to follow him.

All along the way, God is using a different calculus. He is aware that we need to make a set of practical decisions to set up our lives. But he is much less concerned about it than we are, and he won't allow our lives to take shape until that shape corresponds to his main work in us, which is our transformation in charity. The period of indecision that we find so difficult may be just what the divine Doctor has ordered for our instruction and healing.

If we are in the midst of a vocation, we may find that the idea we had of what this would look and feel like is radically different from what we are encountering. We didn't expect this from marriage; we had no idea about that aspect of family life; our dreams of what our life in the convent or at the parish have not materialized; the career that seemed so alluring when we approached it has turned out much less satisfying than we hoped. We then wonder if we heard God at all, and we fret and get discouraged, feeling ourselves trapped in a set of commitments and relationships that don't correspond to our understanding of success. We feel as though we are failing, or that God has failed us.

And all the time God is using exactly these circumstances to accomplish the one thing that will mark true success: he is training us to love. Our notions of a successful life are often seriously inadequate to the depth of that task.

Paul expresses this truth with astonishing clarity in the famous passage about love from the first letter to the Corinthians that we have already mentioned. The passage is so often sentimentalized that it can lose its real meaning. But Paul is being brutally frank about the primacy of charity. The love he speaks about is the opposite of pleasant feelings. For him, as for Christ, the God-given form of love is crucifixion, a "living sacrifice" (Rom 12:1). To love is to be crucified with Christ, to put self and all its illusions to death, so that we can share in the new life that follows.

> If I speak in the tongues of men and of angels, but have not love, I am a noisy gong or a clanging cymbal. And if I have prophetic powers, and understand all mysteries and all knowledge, and if I have all faith, so as to remove mountains, but have not love, I am nothing. If I give away all I have, and if I deliver my body to be burned, but have not love, I gain nothing. (1 Cor 13:1–3)

After listing eminently good qualities and achievements, beyond what most will accomplish, Paul then says, not merely that such accomplishments do not tell the whole tale of success, which would be reasonable enough; but rather that without love, without charity, they are precisely nothing. Paul is not using poetic hyperbole. He is restating the two great commandments of Jesus. The successful life is the life characterized by love. There is no other measure. A life with every possible excellence but lacking love is an utter and complete failure. An excruciatingly painful life, dogged by failure, haunted by suffering, but filled with love, is a glorious success.

- If I attend the best schools and universities and graduate with high honors but have not love;

- If I am a dedicated professional and help many people through my work and win numerous awards but have not love;

- If I have a notable career and retire amid applause and esteem but have not love:

- If I make a lot of money and give large portions of it away but have not love;

- If I marry and stay faithfully married my whole life but have not love;

- If I raise and provide for a large family and see my children into adulthood but have not love;

- If I am well-liked and respected and often consulted for advice but have not love;

✴ If I see notable successes in my service to God but have not love; then I have nothing, and I am nothing.

This is the literal truth.

God, who is not content that we be nothing, carefully arranges the circumstances of our lives that we might learn to love, which means to die to ourselves. The sooner we tear up the images of success that come from this world and learn to embrace God's calculus of success, fleshed out in the life of Christ and echoed in the lives of the saints, the more clearly we will be able to discern and embrace our vocation.

The Second Question: Whom has God given me to love?

We tend to think of a vocation as something that we need to find, something that is out in front of us to be discovered and then lived. There is a truth to this, but it needs to be balanced by another truth: if we are Christians, we are already in the midst of our vocation. We do not need to go find it, though it will no doubt unfold in particular ways over time. We should avoid the spiritually dangerous position of thinking that we are in vocational limbo if the details of life are not quickly setting up. Many young adults find themselves tempted to think this way, as do also those who are in the midst of a change of career, or whose relational lives have been significantly altered.

Whom has God given me to love? To answer this question is to arrive at our vocation. But it is important to make the question current. Not, whom has God given me to love at some future date; but who are those placed in my life right now so that I might love them? The easiest people to love are those who are not around at the moment. Those who live only in our imaginations are the easiest to love of all.

The first and most important answer to this question, who am I to love, will always be: the living God. The call to love the immortal and invisible God, who is the source of life and joy and existence at the heart of all things, is our great longing and our eternal destiny. This love comes before and will outlast every earthly duty and every task and occupation and relationship. In embracing our true vocation, this is always the first and most important question: Do I love God? Put differently, this asks, do I follow his commandments? Does my life properly belong to him? Does he come first? If this posture of love of God is not in place, there is no possibility for the further details of our true vocation to emerge.

The supremacy of the call to love God helps us understand what otherwise would be an insoluble mystery. Typical images of this-worldly success involve at a minimum the necessity of living long enough to experience life's potentialities: to accomplish a set of tasks, to establish a family, to experience the world's joys and sorrows, to excel at an art or a skill. But according to such a standard, most humans have never had the opportunity for success. The majority who come into existence never reach adulthood; and of those who do, only a small minority have the resources, health, and circumstances to order their lives "successfully." It would seem that the vast number of people who die young or in the womb, or who live in circumstances of suffering and limitation, are doomed to a meaningless life. This has caused many to wonder how the world could be created and sustained by a loving God. But what if such categories of success have missed the entire point of our earthly lives? Who knows how God might accomplish his purpose of bringing love to flower in lives that are very short, or characterized by great suffering?

After God: then who?

Those whom our duty calls us to love: members of our family, our friends, those we work with or sit in class with, fellow parishioners, people in our neighborhood, the suffering and the needy. It can be a good meditative exercise to walk through our life and to ask, in the midst of the many people we inevitably run across, whom we might be especially called to love.

Our pride and love of comfort will have us wanting to choose the ones we love. We look for people who think like us, who put us at our ease, whose presence is a blessing rather than a burden. This is natural enough, but there is nothing praiseworthy or transformative about it. "If you love those who love you, what reward have you?" (Mt 5:46). Genuine love receives those God gives, and in the manner God gives. This is why the family, when properly embraced, is a school of love. Spouses, true enough, choose each other, up to a point. But there is hardly a couple who have been married more than a few years who will not say that the person they married and the person they thought they married are two very different people. Parents do not choose their children; they "welcome the stranger" by embracing those God sends them. Children have no choice in their parents, or in their brothers and sisters. In all these relationships, our task is to love those we have been given to love, even where it is difficult. When we have learned to love in this way, overcoming natural preferences and hindrances, we are then placed in a wider field and we bring the practice of genuine love to those around us, and so transform the world. If we love only those whom we find easy to love, we transform nothing. The current tendency toward "designer families"—the children we want with the characteristics we want when we want and in the number we want—has little to do with love.

The same is true in the Church. When Jesus chose the twelve apostles, he did not ask Peter and Andrew whether they liked Thomas, or what James thought of Matthew as a prospective brother. He did the choosing, and it was for them to learn to love those they were yoked with in the new Kingdom. Genuine love always works this way. Those who are learning to love only want to know: where is the altar of sacrificial love that God has prepared for me?

We will find that in whatever state of life or circumstances we are in, God has given us people to love. Not just in the future, but right now. We may not have noticed them yet. They are often not those we would have chosen ourselves; but that is part of the point.

The Third Question: What are the specific contours of my call to love?

Having once understood the inner nature of our call to love, we can then meaningfully ask further questions concerning its practical shape. Am I called to some form of celibacy or to marriage? What should my career or my service be? How should I marshal my energies and my abilities for love? But unless we have understood these questions as rooted in and expressive of the deeper call to love, our discernment will either remain stubbornly murky or will end in an altogether erroneous path. Every specific vocation is an expression of this one vocation: the call to be transformed in love.

How to discern these practical aspects of a vocation is an important and involved question. It is not the point of this discussion, but a few general principles might be mentioned.

THE THREE CALLS

God is ever calling; he constantly knocks on our hearts, leading us into deeper life and fuller obedience. In sorting out the specific contours of a vocation, it may help to consider the three distinctive calls from God, each of which brings a set of possibilities and duties in response.

The First Call

The first call is the universal and irresistible call into being. When God said, let there be light, and land and water, and living things, and the human race, he was issuing this call. The call from nothingness into being is the most fundamental of all: without it we would not be talking about anything else. This call is an ongoing one. The Word of God, the Divine Son, "upholds the universe by his word of power" (Col 1:17). Death is fearsome to us because it drags us back toward the nothingness out of which we came.

None of us cooperated in this call into being; the idea itself makes no sense. God could not discuss with us, before we existed, the possibility of bringing us into existence. We do have the choice, once we are alive and conscious of self, either to embrace our lives as a gift or to rebel against this call and to throw our lives away. The duty of hospitality is an expression of the importance of honoring this call with reverence. We give food and shelter to others as a way of expressing our joy that they are alive, and of contributing to that continued life. From this first call into existence arises all that has to do with sustaining genuine human life, much of which the Church has gathered under the title, Catholic Social Thought.

Certain aspects of vocation come directly from this first call, such as the call to social life, to a just society, and to marriage and family. They are rooted in our created nature, and are the patrimony and responsibility of all humans.

The Second Call

The second call is issued to a fallen race; it is a call back from death to new life, to a share in the Divine Being. Like the first call into being, the second call is also universal: it goes out to the whole human race, to "all the nations." But unlike the first call, it can be resisted. Many are called; fewer respond and are chosen. Peter speaks of this call in his first letter: "You are a chosen race, a royal priesthood, a holy nation, God's own people, that you may declare the wonderful deeds of him who called you out of darkness into his marvelous light"(1 Pet 2:9–10).

The Second Vatican Council emphasized the demands of this call in speaking of the "universal call to holiness." Our duties as Christian disciples involve responding in various ways to the call to become God's children: worshiping him as he has directed, embracing the truths of the faith, living the life of love with others; and proclaiming his Gospel to those around us.

For most of us, discerning our vocation will mean bringing to specificity these two calls. We do not need an additional call to worship God; but we do need to decide where and with whom: this parish, in this capacity, with these people. We do not need to hear the voice of God telling us to go to work for a living; but we need to determine, amid many possibilities, which path of work we should take. We should not wait for a special revelation to begin serving those around us who are in need; but we will have to sort out who among the needy we should concentrate our service upon. We do not need to hear God call us individually to get married; that call comes to us in our creation. But we will need to decide whom we should marry, and when, and whether there are duties or circumstances facing us that may make marriage either impossible or imprudent.

The Third Call

The third call is the call to some form of consecration: priesthood, religious life, or lay celibacy. It is both limited and resistible. Paul refers to this kind of call at the beginning of his letter to the Romans: "Paul, a servant of Jesus Christ, called to be an apostle, set apart for the gospel of God" (Rom 1:1). This call to be "set apart" is issued to certain people, chosen by God for his own mysterious reasons, from among those who have already embraced the call to new life and holiness. This third call needs to be heard individually; to attempt such a life without a specific summons would be to act presumptuously. It is a call out of the naturally graced life of family and career to a supernaturally graced life for the service of God and his people. It is bound by a tighter rule as a result, and a special obedience always characterizes it. It will be clear that this call does not come to those who are better, or more serious about their faith, or more talented than others. A look at the Twelve Apostles puts that idea to rest.

VOCATION AND FREEDOM

For those not called to a form of celibacy, once the primacy of love is established there is room for prudence and free choice in making our vocation specific. We can sometimes think that our future involves one path that we need to find, and that every other path is a mistake that will end in disaster. This is true as regards the basic demands of love—living according to God's commandments, serving those he gives us, and seeking him in prayer. To wander from these is to get lost. But it is different when we are sorting out questions of marriage and family and career and service. The Father wants grown children, not slaves. "No longer do I call you servants, for the servant does not know what his master is doing; but I have called you friends, for all that I have heard from my Father I have made known to you" (Jn 15:15). Those who are friends of Jesus are no less solicitous to obey the one they call Master and Lord; but they do so as knowing their Master's mind. They apply the mind of Christ to the choice of their marriage partner or their career or their place of service. This does not mean that they won't from time to time receive specific guidance for one path over another, but they will not need such guidance to go confidently forward. They know that their Father's delight is that they be of one mind with him, and they aspire to make history in union with him.

The freedom God allows us in establishing the specifics of our vocation is both encouraging and frightening. It is encouraging to know of God's confidence in us, and to know that if we are seeking to be guided by his mind, we can be confident in our choices. But it also means that we cannot hide our fear of responsibility behind a cloak of obedience. If God tells me to do something, I no longer have to take responsibility for it. But this is the sort of responsibility God often wants to dignify us with. Augustine's famous but often misapplied words point to this truth: "Love, and do what you will." He does not mean that it doesn't matter what we do as long as we feel loving or have good intentions. He means that if love of God and neighbor, true self-emptying charity, are at the root of our lives and our actions, then the grace of God will have touched our wills, and our choices will be made according to the mind of Christ. It will be not we who live, but Christ who lives in us.

Discerning the details of our vocation can take time. Those who understand this will not be bound to a schedule based on this-worldly expectations of success. They will avoid the notion that they cannot get their lives underway until all the details are set in place. The vocation to love is always present and available to us. And every vocation this side of heaven is highly tentative, and may have run its course by tomorrow.

The Third Foundation: Vocation

— NOTES —

CHAPTER 9

≈   ≈

THE FOURTH FOUNDATION OF TRUE LEADERSHIP: GIFTS

"What Have I Been Given?"

What have you that you did not receive? If then you received it, why do you boast as if it were not a gift?

1 CORINTHIANS 4:7

As each has received a gift, employ it for one another, as good stewards of God's varied grace: whoever speaks, as one who utters oracles of God; whoever renders service, as one who renders it by the strength which God supplies; in order that in everything God may be glorified through Jesus Christ.

1 PETER 4:10

WE HAVE LOOKED at conviction, character, and vocation as the first three foundations of true leadership. The fourth foundation is gift. Here we ask: what is a gift? or, what do we mean when we speak of identifying our gifts?

Humans were created by God to be interdependent. None of us have all that it takes to live and flourish. We need one another. A gift is a grace, whether of temperament or talent or circumstance or spiritual aptitude,

≈   101

that God has placed within us for the good of others and the building of the Kingdom.

Our gifts are not primarily gifts of God *to* us; they are gifts from God to others *through* us. If we behave as though our gifts belong to us, we rob others and dishonor God. Given how irrational it is to take pride in our gifts and to claim them for our own, it is remarkable how common a failing this is. What do we have that was not given to us? Nonetheless, like the Corinthians Paul was writing to, we have a fatal propensity to boast of our gifts, to evaluate ourselves and others on the basis of their seeming importance, and either to strut proudly because we know ourselves to possess them or to lose confidence and think ourselves unfortunate because we fear we do not possess them. We honor those who have great gifts and we look down on those with few. We assign personal worth, ours and others', on the basis of gifts. To think this way is to be taught by a fallen world. In the Kingdom, gifts show the generosity and thoughtfulness of the giver, not the superiority of the recipient. Compared to the excellence and perfection of God, compared even to the restored beings God intends us one day to be, the most gifted person who has ever lived is very much on a level with the least gifted. We mark such distinctions because we lack the true perspective that the mind of Christ would give us.

Everyone is gifted in various ways and uniquely. Part of our formation as true leaders is to gain self-understanding, to determine what gifts we have been given so that we might rightly exercise them on behalf of others, and along with this to aid others in the exercise of their gifts for the common good.

There are different types of gifts. For our discussion, we might give them a rough and ready description by dividing them into these four broad categories: spiritual gifts, natural gifts, circumstances of life, and, as a special subset of natural gifts, gifts of personality and temperament.

The Fourth Foundation: Personal Gifts

SPIRITUAL GIFTS

Spiritual gifts are those that come to us with new life in Christ, by virtue of the Holy Spirit dwelling in us. That divine presence comes with gifts and powers, given differently to each. In addition to the gifts of faith, hope and love, the Church has long identified the seven gifts of the Holy Spirit listed in Isaiah's eleventh chapter: wisdom, understanding, counsel, fortitude, knowledge, piety, and fear of the Lord. There are the charismatic gifts addressed by Paul in his first letter to the Corinthians, notable among them prophecy, healing, and speaking in tongues. In Romans, Paul gives another listing: "Having gifts that differ according to the grace given to us, let us use them: if prophecy, in proportion to our faith; if service, in our serving; he who teaches, in his teaching; he who exhorts, in his exhortation; he who contributes, in liberality; he who gives aid, with zeal; he who does acts of mercy, with cheerfulness" (Rom 12:6).

The principle so often mentioned by Thomas Aquinas that "grace builds on nature" is in operation here. While some spiritual gifts seem entirely supernatural, many have the same or similar names as virtues, such as wisdom (prudence) and fortitude (courage), and are not unconnected to them: spiritual gifts aid us in developing virtues. The main difference between a virtue and a gift is that while a virtue begins in our human nature and works upward toward perfection through practice, spiritual gifts are graces that come directly from God and increase our aptitude and readiness for a given virtue. Gifts and virtues then meet.

"Make love your aim," writes Paul, "and earnestly desire the spiritual gifts" (1 Cor 14:1). Spiritual gifts enable us to do what otherwise we could not; they bring with them the grace and power of God. Paul makes explicit the other-centered point of such gifts when he encourages the Corinthians to desire them in the context of self-emptying love. "To each is given the manifestation of the Spirit for the common good" (1 Cor 12:7).

NATURAL GIFTS

By natural gifts we mean those that were given us when we were created, what are often called talents. Some are particularly gifted intellectually, or musically, or in regard to physical strength, charm of personality, athletic ability, or administrative capacity. It is when we are dealing with our natural gifts that we are most apt to become wrongly possessive. We selfishly ride our gifts to fame or money or popularity or power, and we call this "living up to our potential." But when God implants gifts in us, he gives them to us on trust, to use according to his purpose. An accountant who treated the revenues of his clients as his personal fortune and spent the money on himself would not be looked upon kindly when the books were examined. So with our natural gifts. They do not belong to us; they belong to God and to those he wants to benefit through us.

While it is true that our natural gifts were given to us to be used for others, it is also true that God is a generous giver, and showers gifts upon us in such measure that we cannot bring all of them to bear during the brief span of a lifetime. Possession of a talent is an indication of possible service to others, but it cannot be a definitive one. The fact that I can play a sport well, or type with great rapidity, doesn't mean that I am called to be an athlete or a secretary. We all have gifts enough for many lifetimes and many different paths; and we are sometimes called to leave the exercise of a particular natural gift for a higher expression of love.

CIRCUMSTANCES OF LIFE

Our circumstances in life are also gifts. Our family situation, the place we hold in society, the particulars of education and relationship we have been given, the time and place into which we were born, all come to us as gifts to be used on behalf of others. Where such circumstances are obviously good when looked at from a this-worldly perspective—a happy home life, a sound education, plenty of financial resources, good health—the gift is clearer. But seen from God's true perspective, even difficult circumstances are meant to be gifts to us and to others. Poverty, sickness, adversity, internal battles with anxiety or depression, while not good in themselves, are transformed by God for those who follow him into sources of grace. "Blessed be the God and Father of our Lord Jesus Christ, the Father of mercies and God of all comfort, who comforts us in all our affliction, so that we may be able to comfort those who are in any affliction, with the comfort with which we ourselves are comforted by God" (2 Cor 1:3). Those who have suffered hardship are uniquely placed to help others in the same position. Many will come to say, after long experience, that their sharp affliction was among the greatest gifts they were given. It is to such people we go when we are in direst need.

Here again, we will need to adjust and correct our understanding such that we perceive our circumstances according to reality, in the light of eternity and the invisible world, instead of looking at this world as the beginning and end of life. This world evaluates circumstances according to what is temporal and seen. The wealthy are fortunate while the poor are marginal; fame is good, obscurity bad. To be well-educated, affluent, powerful, comfortable, and secure, is to be successful. Those who are handed such circumstances at birth are envied, those who attain them by exertion are admired, and those who lack them are disrespected or pitied. But to view things this way is to be caught by an illusion. Who we will one day be, what position or possessions may be ours, has nothing to do with our circumstances here, only with how we handle those circumstances. We are like actors on a stage who have been given costumes and roles to play for a brief time. The question that will determine our future is not what role we happen to have, but how we play it. The point is to view our circumstances, whatever they may be, as a kind of gift in trust, as having potential to be used by God for others.

PERSONALITY AND TEMPERAMENT

Last in this list come our temperaments, our personality type. According to a long tradition that began with the Greeks, a temperament describes an inner orientation that instinctively interacts with the world in a particular way. The classic description of human temperaments identifies four, present in individuals in more or less mixed form: the choleric, the sanguine, the phlegmatic, and the melancholic. Every temperament is a gift and brings with it possibilities and propensities as well as limitations; different temperaments tend to gravitate to certain kinds of roles and activities they are most suited to. Understanding our temperament and learning how different temperaments work can help give us, in broad lines, a sense for how we can best situate ourselves in leadership, and how we best understand and cooperate with others. There are many resources available for gaining a good understanding of temperaments.

IDENTIFYING GIFTS

While we usually have some sense of where our gifts lie, for various reasons our self-understanding can be distorted, and needs to be purified. There are various means to help us identify our gifts.

One among these means is to examine our good desires. We naturally tend toward what we do well; we gravitate toward what we have a gift for. A good starting point in identifying our gifts is to ask: what is it that I like to do? What are the situations and roles that seem most natural to me? What type of environment inspires me, and what type deflates me? This is not an altogether sufficient test: we sometimes like what we have little gift for, and we may not prefer to exercise our true gifts. We may be drawn to what is safe or comfortable, rather than to what will bring our gifts into play. Especially in those areas where we know ourselves to be weak or lacking in character, caution is necessary in sorting out whether our desire is pointing us toward our true gifts. Nonetheless, our desires are a good initial indication of our gifts. There is a false but not uncommon idea that duty is necessarily distasteful, and that if we like what we are doing we are probably doing the wrong thing. Our desires, when not sinful or tending to vanity, are a clue to our gifts. The more fully the image of Christ is formed in us, the more we can trust our desires.

A second means of identifying our gifts is to examine our personal history. Gifts tend to emerge and make themselves known over time. As we look thoughtfully at what we have been drawn to or what we have done well, we can gain clues as to where our gifts lie. Here again, while useful, this means of identifying our gifts is insufficient in itself. This is so especially when we are still young, and haven't had the time or experience to measure our gifts accurately. Some gifts require a certain level of human maturity before they make themselves felt. A gift can lay hidden for a time, and be brought into play by a new environment or a changed set of circumstances.

Yet another important means of identifying our gifts is to pay attention to what others tell us. We are unable to see ourselves well, and others can cure us of our illusions and encourage us in our timidities. An important aspect of friendship among leaders is speaking to each other truly, helping one another to see who we are and what we have been given. We need the courage to speak to others when it is appropriate, and to receive what others say to us.

A fourth means of identifying our gifts is by taking a personality test or gift inventory. There are many of these on offer. While one does not want to rely too much on a blunt instrument for a delicate operation, such tests can give us the broad lines of our temperament and personality and can be a considerable help to us.

GIFTS AND LEADERSHIP

It is a general rule that we should expect to lead, to exercise influence, through the gifts we have been given. We can sometimes fall under the burden of thinking the opposite: that if we are rightly to develop as leaders, we need to place ourselves in situations that call for gifts we do not have. To concentrate only on what we do well can seem to be a failure of self-development. There is a truth in this, but it needs to be rightly moderated. To get out of our comfort zone can be important, especially if laziness or fear are keeping us from exercising our gifts. But this concern to seek challenging and uncomfortable occasions for leadership can be overdone. The ease we experience in exercising a gift is often a sign that we are in the right place. Our gifts tend to increase the influence we exercise. When we lead from strength, we are happier and more at peace, and it is easier for others to receive what we have to offer. No one can expect to exercise their gifts all the time or in all aspects of leadership; sometimes the tasks that God gives us do not seem the most natural or best fitted to us. But in general we should aim for leadership roles that put our gifts to use.

LEARNING TO VIEW GIFTS RIGHTLY

Dealing rightly with our gifts and those of others often requires a radical shift in attitude. As we come to understand rightly the purpose of gifts, we will try to gain as clear and honest an assessment of our gifts as we can, and do our best to find the proper place of exercising influence through them. We will avoid basing our worth or another's dignity on the possession or lack of possession of a particular gift.

Those who think of gifts as possessions for personal enhancement will tend to honor gifts that are highly prized by our society and to dislike those that are denigrated. They will cultivate an unhealthy desire to possess the honored ones, and they will resist the possibility that their gifts may lie elsewhere. They will envy those more gifted than they are; they will accept flattery when it confirms them in their desired gift set, and they will resent being told the truth about themselves if it runs counter to their chosen self-image.

Sometimes this attitude is expressed concerning what is vain and ultimately worthless: good looks, superficial popularity, fame, the right friends. At other times and more subtly it comes into play around genuinely beneficial gifts, of intelligence or competence or spiritual strength. In such a case, when someone else exercises such a gift well, rather than being grateful for the gift, those who hold this attitude become annoyed that they do not possess the same gift, and they harbor a secret dislike for the person who has seemingly put them into the shade.

There are people ambitious for positions of high authority, but who have no aptitude for them. There are others who have leadership gifts that should place them in positions of significant leadership for the common good, but who dislike the responsibility and hard work such positions entail, and so avoid them. Some are attracted to a particular set of gifts: they want to be thought insightful, or exotic, or clever, or super-organized, or everyone's best friend. They then go to great lengths to practice their chosen pose. We can convince ourselves that we are good at something that in fact we have no aptitude for, and others may not have the heart to tell us the truth, because they know it will devastate us. Yet the truth should never be devastating; it should always be liberating, because it will enable us better to use what has been lodged in us for the sake of others.

It is a common tendency to think that the gifts we have been given are of less importance than those we do not have. We can see the difference made by the exercise of another's gift; but because we are unable to see clearly the difference made by our own gifts, we think that what we bring is of little importance. In this matter of gifts, familiarity can breed contempt. The one who is gifted in consistent and competent work wishes he could express creative brilliance instead. The one who refreshes those around her with the gift of a joyful and gregarious personality regrets that she isn't mysterious and fascinating. The one whose gift of loyalty and whose team spirit animates an operation and secures its success is disappointed that he doesn't have what it takes to be in charge. This sort of attitude can rob us of proper confidence in the exercise of our gifts. Rather, we want to embrace the person God has created us to be, and to desire the perfections implicit in that person, rather than dissipating our energies by wishing ourselves different from what we are. We know that our fundamental worth and our true identity have nothing to do with our gifts.

CULTIVATING THE GIFTS OF OTHERS

There is a kind of leader who exercises impressive gifts, but in a way that suppresses and suffocates the gifts of others. There is another kind of leader who by her manner of leadership makes herself necessary and irreplaceable. These are faulty exercises of leadership. They betray a problematic self-focus and a lack of proper concern for the cultivation of others' gifts. Much of the exercise of leadership involves helping those around us to identify and cultivate their gifts such that they can be of most use to others. A true leader makes a study of his own and others' gifts, not selfishly or critically, but in order to bring those gifts rightly into play.

⋮ ⋮ ⋮

Gaining a healthy attitude to our gifts and those of others brings freedom and joy to leadership. Among the unfortunate effects of the radical individualism of our culture is the idea that each of us stands alone, and that therefore we all should to be able to do everything well. We can labor under an unrealistic self-expectation that leaves us anxious and paralyzed in the face of our limitations. The liberating truth is that we are not meant to carry the challenge and burden of life by ourselves. We are members of a body, and the gifts given to others are meant to help us along the way. The more we see this truth, the easier it will be to find joy in the strengths and gifts of those around us, and the readier we will be to offer to others the gifts that God has lodged in us for the common good.

— NOTES —

CHAPTER 10

CONVICTION AND CHARACTER
IN RELATION TO GIFTS

*Then I said, "Ah, Lord God! Behold, I do not know how to speak, for
I am only a youth." But the Lord said to me, "Do not say, 'I am only a
youth'; for to all to whom I send you you shall go, and whatever I command you you shall speak. Be not afraid of them, for I am with you to
deliver you, says the Lord."*

JEREMIAH 1:6–8

CONVICTION, CHARACTER, AND gifts are all foundations of true
leadership; each has great importance. But as important as gifts are, conviction and character are more important still. Current thinking about
leadership is so focused on identifying and exercising gifts, and pays
comparatively so little attention to the obedience of faith and the development of character, that it can be worth hammering the point home.
This will not be taken to mean that gifts are insignificant, only that they
need to be viewed in their proper context. Gifts are tools, wielded by a
person of character guided by conviction. A sharp sword is an effective
weapon, but in the hands of an unskilled swordsman becomes dangerous to himself and others; strong gifts in the grip of weak character or
lack of conviction can overthrow their possessor and lead to disaster. The

Scriptures go to great lengths to insist on this point. Let us look at a few concrete examples.

KING SAUL

Among the most tragic examples of great gifts spoiled by lack of proper conviction and character is found in Israel's first king, Saul.

The Israelites, chafing against the oppression of the Philistines, demanded that the prophet Samuel anoint a king for them. Against Samuel's advice, they determined to have a king like the nations around them, believing this was the only way to win their freedom. They saw this as a political and military necessity: it was the responsibility of kings to defend their people and fight their battles. Samuel, directed by God to accede to their wishes, anointed Saul as Israel's first king.

Saul had many impressive gifts. His first and greatest gift was to be chosen by God and given the spiritual gift of kingship. "Samuel took a vial of oil and poured it on his [Saul's] head, and kissed him and said, 'Has not the Lord anointed you to be prince over his people Israel? And you shall reign over the people of the Lord and you will save them from the hand of their enemies round about. And this shall be the sign to you that the Lord has anointed you to be prince over his heritage'" (1 Sam 10:1). Saul was given his kingship, not by Samuel, but by God himself. He did not seize his crown by violence or intrigue against a host of contenders; he did not plot to overthrow an existing king; he did not set himself to gain power out of personal ambition. He was chosen by another, and he came to the throne peacefully, backed by all the authority of God himself. Because God had called him to the position, Saul could expect God to provide the necessary strength and resources for his success. Despite serious external challenges, Saul began his task of leadership under excellent circumstances.

Saul was physically imposing: tall and attractive, he looked the part of a king. "There was not a man among the people of Israel more handsome than he; from his shoulders upward he was taller than any of the people" (1 Sam 9:2). This may seem a superficial quality, but for a king who was initiating a new rule, who did not come by his kingship through long custom, appearance was important. He needed to gain the confidence of a people who had not known him as king and were not in the habit of being ruled. When Samuel presented Saul to the Israelites, Samuel made much of this, evidently to great effect. "Samuel said to all the people, 'Do you see him whom the Lord has chosen? There is none like him among all the people.' And all the people shouted, 'Long live the king!'" (1 Sam 10:24).

Saul was an excellent warrior, able and courageous. He came from the stock of Benjamin, a tribe famous for its prowess in battle. His task was a difficult one: the Philistines had thousands of chariots, a large cavalry, and were well-equipped for war, while Saul had far fewer men, none of whom had so much as swords or spears. And there were other nations besides the Philistines that were hostile to an emerging Israelite power. Yet he prevailed against them all. "When Saul had taken the kingship over Israel, he fought against all his enemies on every side, against Moab, against the Ammonites, against Edom, against the kings of Zobah, and against the Philistines; wherever he turned he put them to the worse. And he did valiantly, and smote the Amalekites, and delivered Israel out of the hands of those who plundered them" (1 Sam 14:47–48). Saul's impressive personal appearance was evidently backed up by a Benjaminite skill in the use of arms. He was given a kingdom in hope, and with the aid of God he battled for and won his kingdom.

Saul was a natural leader. He was the kind of captain men love to follow. He had the confident leader's sure touch in gaining a following: he knew how to bring able men under his leadership. "There was hard fighting against the Philistines all the days of Saul; and when Saul saw any strong man, or any valiant man, he attached him to himself" (1 Sam 14:52).

Saul also had good qualities of temperament and character. He was not without faith in God. He wanted to rule under God's lordship, and was concerned for proper worship. His initial approach to the throne was marked by a praiseworthy modesty: like many who would later be called to high honors in the Church, his first reaction to the possibility of kingship was to hide himself.

Nonetheless he failed, and his kingdom was taken from him. Was his failure due to a lack of gift? No, it was more fundamental: it was a failure of character and of faith: he was disobedient. Not acknowledging that his kingship was a participation in the rule of God and that its success demanded a watchful waiting upon God's commands, he came to fear human opinion more than God's decrees. How Saul came to his crisis is an involved story: enough for our purposes to note that, overcome by fear and lacking faith, he failed the leader's test of obedience. "Samuel said to Saul, 'You have done foolishly; you have not kept the commandment of the Lord your God, which he commanded you; for now the Lord would have established your kingdom over Israel forever. But now your kingdom shall not continue; the Lord has sought out a man after his own heart; and the Lord has appointed him to be prince over his people, because you have not kept what the Lord commanded you'" (1 Sam 13:12–13).

This greatly gifted man, who began so well and with such seemingly good intentions, ended in failure. Because Saul did not have God's heart, because he did not seek God's mind and character, he saw all the high promise of his youth vanish, and he watched as his kingdom was torn away from him. As he grew older he became increasingly tormented by an evil spirit, gnawed at by jealousy and fear, and even began to fight against God by trying to kill the man God had anointed in his place. He came to a miserable end committing suicide rather than be captured by his Philistine enemies. Too late, Saul admitted to Samuel the nature of his fault. "I have transgressed the commandment of the Lord and your words, because I feared the people and obeyed their voice" (1 Sam 15:24).

SOLOMON

The catalogue of Solomon's gifts is extensive and extraordinary. There has hardly ever been such a combination of natural aptitude, supernatural graces, and promising circumstance.

Unlike Saul, and unlike David who took Saul's place, Solomon did not need to fight for his kingdom; it was handed to him in peace. He benefited from the battles of those two "men of blood," and he enlarged and consolidated the kingdom he had been given. "Judah and Israel were as many as the sand by the sea; they ate and drank and were happy. Solomon ruled over all the kingdoms from the Euphrates to the land of the Philistines and to the border of Egypt; they brought tribute and served Solomon all the days of his life" (1 Kgs 4:20–22).

Solomon was wise even as a youth, and when given by God the choice of whatever he wanted, with a rare wisdom he requested that he be given yet deeper wisdom. God was pleased with the choice, and settled upon him a supernatural gift surpassing anything that had yet been known. "God gave Solomon wisdom and understanding beyond measure, and largeness of mind like the sand on the seashore, so that Solomon's wisdom surpassed the wisdom of all the people of the east, and all the wisdom of Egypt. And men came from all peoples to hear the wisdom of Solomon, and from all the kings of the earth, who had heard of his wisdom" (1 Kgs 4:29–30; 34).

The Queen of the South paid a visit to Solomon, and was overwhelmed by what she encountered. She rightly saw that Solomon's prosperity and the glory of his court were gifts from the hand of God.

> When the queen of Sheba had seen all the wisdom of Solomon, the house that he had built, the food of his table, the seating of his officials, and the attendance of his servants, their clothing, his cupbearers, and his burnt offerings which he offered at the house of the Lord, there was no more spirit in her. And she said to the king, "The

report was true which I heard in my own land of your affairs and of your wisdom, but I did not believe the reports until I came and my own eyes had seen it; and, behold, the half was not told me; your wisdom and prosperity surpass the report which I heard. Happy are your wives! Happy are these your servants, who continually stand before you and hear your wisdom! Blessed be the Lord your God, who has delighted in you and set you on the throne of Israel! Because the Lord loved Israel for ever, he has made you king, that you may execute justice and righteousness." (1 Kgs 10:1–9)

But though God gave Solomon gifts of peaceful rule and fabulous wealth and unparalleled knowledge and wisdom, all did not go well. Solomon served God well while he was young, and built a temple for his worship and sought wisdom at his hands; but in the end his wisdom was overthrown by a false heart.

For when Solomon was old his wives turned away his heart after other gods; and his heart was not wholly true to the Lord his God, as was the heart of David his father. For Solomon went after Ashtoreth the goddess of the Sidonians, and after Milcom the abomination of the Ammonites. So Solomon did what was evil in the sight of the Lord, and did not wholly follow the Lord, as David his father had done.... And the Lord was angry with Solomon, because his heart had turned away from the Lord, the God of Israel by a heart that was not fully given to God." (1 Kgs 11:4–6; 8–10)

Centuries later, the Israelites were still marveling at the greatness and the fall of Solomon:

How wise you became in your youth! You overflowed like a river with understanding. Your soul covered the earth, and you filled it with parables and riddles. Your name reached to far-off islands, and you were loved for your peace. In the name of the Lord God, who is called the God of Israel, you gathered gold like tin and amassed silver like lead. But you laid your loins beside women, and through your body you were brought into subjection. You put a stain upon your honor, and defiled your posterity, so that you brought wrath upon your children, and they were grieved at your folly, so that the sovereignty was divided and a disobedient kingdom arose out of Ephraim. (Sir 47:14ff)

The fruit of Solomon's failure was loss of peace with foreign enemies and a civil war that divided the Israelite kingdom and robbed from it the unity intended by God. Solomon's sin was the beginning of Israel's apostasy and eventual ruin. Such was the unworthy end of a supremely gifted and excellently circumstanced man.

THE DEVIL

The clearest example of gift without the proper heart, that is, without conviction and character, is found in that angelic being who came to be called Satan, the adversary and accuser of the human race. Created greatest of all the angels, he is the most gifted creature who has ever lived. His gifts of intelligence and beauty and strength must have been overwhelming to have enabled him to lead so many angels away from the light of God. Yet he became enamored by his own beauty, and rejecting the image of God within himself, he chose to be independent of God, and to set himself in God's place. Created to reflect the majesty and goodness of God with unparalleled intensity, he instead chose pride, and failed miserably, and implicated myriads of others in his failure.

"How you are fallen from heaven, O Day Star, son of Dawn! How you are cut down to the ground, you who laid the nations low!" (Is 14:12). The devil, even today, is the most influential personality on the face of the earth apart from Christ alone. By his craftiness and subtlety and power, he is still able to get much of mankind to follow him. But he is not a true leader. His gifts, such as they are in a corrupted state, are now employed for evil rather than for good. According to the old Latin saying, *corruptio optimi pessima*: the corruption of the best becomes the worst; the fall of the highest leads to the lowest.

There is an important principle of leadership here. God endows his creatures with gifts so that they can bring about goodness through them. If those gifts become corrupted by a false heart, they do not lose all their power, but their exercise leads to evil rather than goodness. To train and cultivate gifts without a corresponding formation in conviction and character is to set loose great evil upon the world.

THE TRIUMPH OF CONVICTION AND CHARACTER

To underline this point about the primacy of faith and character in relation to gifts, the Scripture gives us numerous examples in which gift was lacking, but faith and character were present, with positive results.

One such example is the patriarch Abraham. He was old; he was a sojourner exiled from his native land; his wife could no longer bear children; yet he was told by God that he was to be father of many nations. On what basis? On gift? No, by faith and obedience. "He did not weaken in faith when he considered his own body, which was as good as dead because he was about a hundred years old or when he considered the barrenness of Sarah's womb. No distrust made him waver concerning the promise of God" (Rom 4:18–20). As a result he accomplished the purpose for which God had called him. "From one man, and him as good as dead, were born descendants as many as the stars of heaven and as the innumerable grains of sand by the seashore" (Heb 11:13).

The moral of the story frequently repeats itself. Moses, a man slow of speech and lacking eloquence, was given the role of a prophet. Gideon, a commander with a few hundred soldiers, was instructed to go to battle against a vast army. Jeremiah thought he was too young; Isaiah declared himself unclean; Elizabeth was beyond childbearing years; and the Blessed Mother had had no relations with a man. In each case it seemed that gift was lacking; in each case the plan of God was fulfilled. God uses the simple to shame the wisdom of the wise.

The clearest example of the preeminence of faith and character over gifts is that of Christ himself. Although supremely, even perfectly gifted in everything, the keystone of the ministry of Jesus was not the impressive exercise of his gifts, but rather faithfulness and obedience to the Father. This principle is seen in Christ's temptation by the devil. The devil took Jesus to a great height and showed him all the kingdoms of the world and the glory of them. "All these I will give you, if you will fall down and worship me" (Mt 4:8). Jesus was fully capable of seizing such worldly power; otherwise this would have been no temptation at all. He had the charisma, the firmness of will, the force of eloquence, the strength of personality, and the spiritual power to take all this for himself. But he turned aside from it, and instead spent his time among the simple and the powerless and the uneducated. Because he emptied himself, the Father exalted him.

⋮ ⋮ ⋮

Gifts are given to us for the good of others, and we should not denigrate or undervalue them. To use our gifts well, according to the plan of God, is best. But we should not overvalue them either. God, who is the giver of gifts, and who gives or withholds at his good pleasure, is fully capable of making up a lack in this area, as the Scripture repeatedly shows. His first demand upon those who follow him is not giftedness, but rather obedience, faithfulness, and Godlike character, so that we who are made in his image can represent him truly and act on his behalf.

TRUE LEADERSHIP

— NOTES —

CHAPTER 11

THE FIFTH FOUNDATION: SKILLS

"How Do I Prepare for Life's Tasks?"

Be neither careless nor tepid. Never permit the children of this world to show greater care and interest in the things of time than you show for those of eternity. It should bring a blush to your cheek to see them run to death more enthusiastically than you to life. Hold yourselves as worth little if a courtier serves with greater dedication to gain the favor of an earthly prince than you do for the favor of the King of Heaven, or if a soldier battles with greater courage for the glory of victory and hope of spoils, than you fight for victory and triumph over the world, the devil, and yourselves, all for a heavenly kingdom and eternal glory.

ST. IGNATIUS LOYOLA

Everyone to whom much is given, of him will much be required; and of him to whom men commit much they will demand the more.

LUKE 12:48

IF WE HAVE left a discussion of leadership skills to the last place, it is not because they are not important. Each of these five foundations is an essential aspect of true leadership, this one no less than the previous four. We have put skills in fifth place, not because honing good leadership skills is unimportant, but because these skills need to be rooted in and guided by the first four foundations. It is a common mistake to think that the essence of good leadership is in perfecting a set of techniques that are more or less mechanical in their operation. Great skill makes the excellent practitioner, but not the true leader. In an age that emphasizes technical skill and undervalues character, it is important to restore the proper balance.

Nonetheless, the true leader puts a high value on developing the skills that allow him or her to participate in Christ's leadership most fully. It can sometimes happen that Christians, who know that God loves them and does not hold them to an impossible standard, can presume upon his kindness and offer a lazy or incompetent service. The idea can subtly take hold that God doesn't really care how well we do our work, as long as we are sincere about it. St. Ignatius thought otherwise. "Be neither careless nor tepid," he wrote to his brothers. In this he was echoing the words of Jesus in the parable of the talents, when the master reprimands the servant who had hidden what had been entrusted to him: "You wicked and slothful servant! You knew that I reap where I have not sowed, and gather where I have not winnowed? Then you ought to have invested my money with the bankers, and at my coming I should have received what was my own with interest. So take the talent from him, and give it to him who has the ten talents" (Mt 25:26–28). To the one given much, much will be required.

Credibility in leadership is gained through a combination of character and competence. If either is seriously lacking, our influence, our leadership, will not be effective. Just as we take seriously the need to gain the character of Christ, so we should take seriously the task of becoming genuinely competent.

Gaining the proper skills for life occupies much of our education. There are as many skills as there are activities and occupations. In general our world is good at imparting skills, and it would be both impossible and unnecessary to catalogue all of them here. But beyond the technical skills needed for particular tasks, there are a set of skills that come into play in any exercise of genuine leadership. In this chapter we will look at some of those. The aim here is to provide a practical checklist, such that those aspiring to true leadership can give these skills proper attention. This is not a complete treatment of them; it is instead a starting point. There are excellent resources available for describing them and their attainment in greater detail.

We have identified three broad areas of important skills: (1) organizing life effectively, (2) communicating well, and (3) leading a team. Basic competence in these skills can and should be mastered by all leaders, whatever their personality or gift.

1. ORGANIZATION OF LIFE

Children rightly have their lives patterned and organized by the adults who care for them. This changes as we grow up. Part of what it means to become an adult is to take responsibility for the organization of our own lives. For those who lead, such responsibility becomes essential. We have a limited amount of time, energy, money, and material resources given us, and it is ours to determine how we use them. There can be a tendency to resist taking responsibility for the organization of our lives, and to remain children beyond the years of childhood. We can allow ourselves to be dominated by external circumstances, or by others' demands upon us. While external factors play a role in the ordering of our time and resources, in the final analysis it is our responsibility to master and manage them.

A common expression of this unwillingness to take responsibility comes in the form of making excuses. "I had a lot going on." "I was not feeling well." "I ran out of time." "I had too many tasks heaped upon me." "I didn't plan for that eventuality." "So-and-so didn't help me." Any or all of these excuses may in a given instance be true, and sometimes need to be taken into account. But a habitual litany of excuses can reveal a basic stance of passivity: I am reacting rather than acting, and it is some-one else's job to see that I don't have more to do than I can reasonably accomplish.

When this passive stance becomes habitual, we settle into the idea that we are not masters of our time and energy. The true leader, on the other hand, cultivates an attitude of responsibility rather than passivity and avoids making excuses even when they might be legitimate.

A key aspect of ordering life is the management of time. We need to learn to use our time as a resource, and not to waste it. Not wasting time does not mean that we spend no time in leisure or relaxation; it is not a recipe for becoming a workaholic. It means rather that we decide how our time will be spent on the basis of thoughtful planning; we apportion our time according to what is most important. For this we need to construct a schedule, for our day, our week, and our year, commensurate with the degree of complexity of our lives and our tasks, and then hold ourselves to it. We need to gain the habit of spending the right amount of time on the right things by setting priorities and seeing that we do not allow unim-portant matters to dominate our time.

There are those who say, "I'm not that type of person. I'm sponta-neous and I just let things happen." This is a bad excuse for incompetence. There are obviously those for whom ordering things comes easily and effortlessly, and others who need to struggle to bring reasonable order out of impending chaos. There are some who tend to establish a too-rigid order and need to learn a more humane way of ordering their own and others' lives lest they suffocate the environments they inhabit. Not every-one will bring order in the same way and to the same degree. But the task of taking responsibility for the time that has been given us is not depen-dent on personality type. We all need to learn the skill of rightly managing time and resources.

There are others who know they need to do better at organizing time and priorities, but who then fall prey to what might be called "binge orga-nizing." Like someone who never exercises and who, under a passing attitude of energy, dives into an intensive program of physical fitness, only to tire of it after a short time and abandon it, they will seize upon one of the many tools on offer and throw themselves into a frenzy of organization. Having made lists and schedules and priorities and systematized them in attractive color schemes, they then find that they hardly glance at the perfect system they have made. Their mistake is not in their desire to be organized; it is rather in forgetting that mastering this kind of skill is a habit gained by practice over time. Learning to organize our time and priorities requires discipline and consistency, like learning to play an instrument or to speak a second language. If we keep at it, realistically and with determination, we will improve.

Here are a few important things to keep in mind as we set about organizing our time:

1. *Make a schedule.*

How often we reproach ourselves by saying that we need to get more exercise, or that we really should be spending more time with certain people, or that we need to do better at giving thought to planning, or that we ought to find more time for prayer or reading or service. Time passes, and nothing changes, and we find ourselves saying the same things over and over. Unless we do the hard work of getting these important activities into a schedule we will spend a lot of time in wishful thinking.

2. *Stick to the schedule once it is made.*

Making a schedule is an important task; but unless we abide by the schedule we have made there is not much point to it. It can happen that we put together a schedule that looks good on paper, but that we find we cannot follow, so we set it aside. Instead we should wrestle with our schedule such that it becomes workable and realistic. If we construct a theoretical schedule that doesn't work, rather than throwing it away we should adjust it until we arrive at a workable one. Much in life is unpredictable, and no schedule can or should prepare us for all eventualities. But the broad outlines of our time can be ordered so that we can properly exercise stewardship of this precious resource.

3. Look over responsibilities and set priorities.

What are the most important ways to spend my time? Determining this is an important part of constructing a schedule. It is a valuable exercise to walk through the many aspects of our lives and the duties they present, in family, work, service, prayer, and social life, and then thoughtfully see that each finds its rightful place, a place represented concretely by the hours, days, and weeks that we assign to it.

4. Periodically revisit and reevaluate the priorities we have set and the schedule we have made.

The contours and tasks of life are constantly changing. This means that we should regularly set aside time to evaluate how our schedule is working, whether it needs changing, and whether our priorities need re-arranging. How often this is done will vary depending on circumstances, but it is good to be specific about when and how often we will do the evaluation, lest it slip away entirely.

5. Allow for the proper place of leisure.

Leisure, rightly understood, is not merely a time to recover after stretches of overwork, or to devote to personally gratifying activities. It is rather a time given to the most important things in life. It provides us an opportunity to be renewed, to put ourselves back into our proper form, to bring ourselves into contact with the deepest human and supernatural sources of our lives. We call leisure "re-creation" because it helps us to restore to its rightful shape, both within ourselves and in our environments, whatever has been deformed by the press of a chaotic world. Leisure needs to be protected in our schedules so that we don't become machine-like, overwhelmed by the routines of the temporal world and forgetful of the true contours of our humanity. The right approach to leisure allows for the right attitude to the rest of life. This is why the Third Commandment of the Decalogue, keeping holy the Lord's Day, has always been understood as the kernel of all true leisurely activity.

2. COMMUNICATING WELL

It is no accident that the educational ideal that built Western civilization is founded on the ability to speak and write clearly and well. The proper use of words, connected as it is to the ability to think well, is close to our understanding of what it means to be human. This is why the disciplines that teach us how to use words have been called "the humanities."

An essential skill for the true leader is competence in the use of language. In every area of life—work and the professions, marriage and family, friendship, worship, and entertainment—ability with language is a great advantage for exercising influence, and incompetence is a serious drawback. Here we find ourselves at a disadvantage. Our current environment is flush with words, but they often come to us in a chaotic form that tends to garble rather than clarify thought. First with emails, then with texting and social media, we have been schooled in sloppy speech. This is not just a matter of bad etiquette, like bringing dirty hands to the dinner table. Words are the medium of our thought. The more words we have at our disposal, and the more accurately and skillfully we use them, the richer and deeper are the possibilities of our thinking, and the more effective we will be at opening our minds to others. Those who have few words and who do not use them well will find themselves hampered and ineffective in much that they attempt.

Here, then, is a short list of aims for gaining competence in the use of language:

1. Do not waste your education.

We should take advantage of our formal education and the opportunities it gives us to learn to write and speak. This means looking upon our reading and writing assignments, not as tasks to get through quickly and then forget, but as opportunities to hone our language skills.

2. Keep to a steady diet of well-written works.

Regularly reading the great masters of the language will increase our ability to write and to speak well. Even if at times we need to wrestle with language that may not be easy for us, our minds and capacities are getting stretched and strengthened in the process. The amount of reading need not be burdensome as long as we keep to it with consistency.

3. Maintain a high standard for the use of language.

We will do well to disengage ourselves from the bad habits that current electronic media tend to foster: the slangy, the sloppy, the overfamiliar, the misspelt, and the grammatically incoherent. Our goal is not to be flowery or artificially formal; it is rather to write clearly and well, and so to become master of our words.

4. Learn how to properly communicate in different settings.

We should gain competence in the different ways of writing or speaking called for in a variety of situations. This means, for instance, getting to know the difference between language appropriate to casual conversation and that required for formal communication. There is a language for written reports, another for oral presentations, another for getting through business in a meeting setting. There are times for brevity, and times for extensive detail. There are modes of speaking and writing appropriate for communicating with a superior, another for collaborating with a colleague, and another for giving directives to those we are leading. There are situations in which it is appropriate to communicate our personal opinions or our emotive responses, and situations in which it is not. In all of this it is good to think of our use of words as a process of gaining mastery of a craft or an art.

5. *Pay special attention to communication with superiors.*
Proper communication with those who lead us is an important aspect of the skill in language noted in the previous item. It is essential for effective work as a team. We should respond promptly to communications from superiors in work or in service, even if it only to say that we have received what they have sent us. Especially given the prevalence of social media, we will want to make a clear distinction between the way we informally communicate with friends and the way we communicate with those we are responsible to.

6. *Learn to speak in front of others with calm and seriousness.*
Difficult as it is, we should seize, rather than avoid, opportunities to speak in front of others. Much of the reason people are so afraid of public speaking is that they have had so little practice at it. With practice and experience comes greater confidence.

In dealing with our competence in language, we need to be careful not to box ourselves into failure by a false self-perception. There are people who have a gift for learning and using language well, and others who have had the benefit of a good training in language skills. If we aren't one of those, if writing and language skills have not come easily to us or if we have not received a good education in them (a common experience in our current situation), we can fall into the attitude of believing that we are just not good at communication, that we never will be, and that it is too late to do anything about it. This is not true. Everyone has the ability to gain basic competence in the use of language, and all of us can significantly improve our language skills as we steadily pursue them.

3. TEAM LEADERSHIP

Leadership necessarily involves us with others. This means that the exercise of leadership demands skill in knowing how to lead a team of people. (By "team" here is meant any group of people gathered together for a common task.) The principle that underlies team leadership is simple: the team leader is responsible for carrying out the given project as a whole, and the team leader's first concern is to see that all members of the team have what they need to accomplish their part in that whole. It stands to reason that more can be accomplished by a well-functioning team than by individuals working haphazardly. Everyone has had good and bad experiences of teamwork. We know the joy of being part of a well-functioning team, and the frustration that comes when it seems that team members are working against each other. The difference between the two experiences has much to do with how the team is led.

The heart of team leadership is service: the team leader is serving other team members for the sake of the common good. A typical temptation for the team leader is to become so absorbed in his or her own work that team members are left in the dark about their roles in the overall project. To overcome this temptation, a disciplined effort is required of the team leader to take a broader view, to put aside self and to see the overall effort rather than confine his attention to his own activities. A telltale sign of this kind of leadership failure is annoyance at interruption. The very business of the team leader is to be interrupted, to be ready to put down what he is doing, to be available to attend to what a member of her team needs. Taking this posture is more than just an effective way to get a job done; it is also an expression of respect toward those being led. If a team leader gets impatient or annoyed at a request for help or direction, that leader is saying, in so many words, "Don't you see that I am busy and that my job is more important than yours?" It can often be perceived as, "Don't you understand that I am more important than you are?" Properly attending to a team not only gets the job done well; it reinforces the truth that the people we lead are more important than the task we and they are accomplishing together.

When the team leader is attentive to team members, seeing that each understands both the overall project and his or her place in contributing to the project's success, team members become more engaged in what they are doing, and can more easily bring their own gifts and creativity to the service of the common project.

There are many skills needed to lead a team well. Here are a few important ones: (1) planning and evaluation, (2) leading and participating in meetings, and (3) giving and receiving praise and correction.

TEAM PLANNING AND EVALUATION

Leading a team effort begins with proper planning. For instance, a person is moving into a new home, and has invited friends to come to help with packing and sorting and loading a truck. The friends arrive ready to pitch in and help. If the person doing the move has planned well, a number of important matters will have been considered: what the "critical path" is for the various tasks at hand; how much time and manpower will be necessary at different stages of the move; what kinds of tools and materials will be needed. The job will likely go smoothly, and it will be an enjoyable and productive afternoon. But if there has been no effort of planning, the move will be an exercise in annoyance: there will be confusion, standing around and wasting time, and interminable discussions about how best to do the job.

What follows is a short checklist for planning and evaluation.

1. *Communicate the overall vision.*

"What are we doing here?" is a question everyone asks, sometimes only implicitly: we need to know that what we are doing is worth our time and trouble. The team leader has the primary responsibility for answering that question: for understanding the purpose of the project, and for finding ways of keeping the vision "in the air" for the rest of the team. A team is animated and energized when the vision is clear, but will become quickly dispirited if the overall point of the common effort grows dim.

2. *Set specific goals that are clear, purposeful, and realistic.*

The team leader needs not only to keep the overall vision of the project before the team members, but also to set specific and limited goals toward its accomplishment that are clear and realizable. Members of a team should know what the team is attempting to accomplish, not only as an overall task, but in its more immediate goals. In keeping with the overall vision, the team leader either sets such goals or establishes the process by which they are arrived at, and then keeps the team focused on those goals. Overall vision and specific goals are essential for the team effort. They provide the framework for setting priorities, for making decisions about planning, and for evaluation. If the vision and the specific goals are well thought through and articulated, the team will tend to function well. If they are not, the common effort will suffer or founder.

3. *Set clear expectations for each team member.*

Once the team goal is in place, it is the task of the team leader to make sure that each team member knows what is expected of him or her. Clear expectations impart confidence and encourage engagement. Vague or unclear expectations are a recipe for anxiety, boredom, or disengagement.

4. *Think through the critical path.*
The team leader determines what needs to be done when and by whom and in what order so that the whole can be accomplished well. The example of the conductor of an orchestra can help: he plays no instrument himself; his task is rather to pay attention to the different sections of the orchestra and to bring them into play at the right moment. So with the team leader, who orchestrates the effort such that each person's contribution is rightly related to the whole, and the common work remains integrated.

5. *Delegate properly.*
The team leader who micro-manages, whether because of anxiety or an exaggerated desire for control or sometimes just because of a tendency to get lost in unimportant details, attempts to do the work of others. This is not only inefficient, but disrespectful. The team leader needs to give team members the necessary room to perform their parts, even to perform them badly, which is an essential part of learning. The team leader who delegates expresses confidence in team members and increases their sense of responsibility for the task. The micro-manager expresses lack of confidence in team members, who then find their enthusiasm and commitment waning. The well-known saying, "If you want something done well, do it yourself" is fine for the lone wolf, but it will not do for a leader of a team.

6. *Evaluate appropriately and in a timely fashion.*
Good evaluation by the team leader is important for good teamwork. It is

important that team members know that they are doing their part well, or if they need to improve, where such improvement lies.

LEADING AND PARTICIPATING IN MEETINGS

Once we have a task that goes beyond individual effort, meetings become necessary. Meetings can take many different forms. Knowing how to organize, lead, and participate in meetings is an important leadership skill. Here are some tips for gaining that skill:

1. A meeting should be purposive.
Meetings are important, but they can be immense time-wasters. We need to avoid the illusion that if many meetings are taking place, much work is getting done. Often the opposite is the case. The rule is: if a meeting is needed, meet. If a meeting is not needed, do not meet. So the first question to ask is, do we need a meeting, and if so, for what purpose?

2. Communicate the purpose of the meeting to the participants.
If the goal of the meeting is clear, participants will know better how to contribute. If the goal is unclear, a meeting can easily drift and become ineffective. The purpose and plan of a meeting is often communicated by giving participants an agenda ahead of time. In less formal situations the communication may be done differently; in any case the leader of a meeting should have planned ahead, should know clearly the point of the meeting, and should communicate this to the participants.

3. Keep the meeting focused and on task.

A competent leader of a meeting will calmly but firmly keep the goal of the meeting in view, and rein in possible distractions. If there is no specific task for a time together (e.g., a social gathering), that should be clear to those present.

4. *Keep your eyes on the common goal, not on the self.*
Both in leading and in participating, the point of meeting is not to put on a performance, nor to outdo another participant, nor to get attention. If a contribution is germane to the stated purpose of the meeting, it should be made. If it is not, it should be left alone or taken up outside the meeting. The point of holding a meeting is to deal with matters that are of concern to all present; participants should resist the temptation to occupy valuable meeting time with matters that would best be handled elsewhere. A meeting is not a convenient place to get one's own work done.

5. *Involve the participation of all who need to contribute.*
The meeting leader should see that all who have something important to bring to the meeting are given the opportunity to make their contribution. It is the task of the meeting leader to order the time together such that it is not only the most aggressive or most talkative who have their say.

6. *Be respectful of others' time and energy.*
An important principle for meetings, whether as leader or participant, is to be respectful of other people's time. As a meeting leader, this means starting and ending on time, and getting through the business of the meeting as quickly as is reasonable. As a meeting participant, this means disciplining oneself by contributing only when necessary, refraining from saying whatever comes to mind, and keeping oneself to the stated purpose of the meeting.

GIVING AND RECEIVING PRAISE
AND CORRECTION

An important but often difficult duty of the team leader is the giving of praise and correction. It is important because it is essential for the quality of the common task and for the proper training and peace of mind of the people involved; it is difficult because it can be a demanding personal interaction that we would often rather avoid.

The first requisite for the team leader in giving encouragement and correction is his or her own ability to receive them well from others. In this, as in all matters, the leader is first a follower. Some important truths are worth repeating in this context: that self-worth does not come from perfect accomplishment of a task; that the more we are looking away from ourselves and toward the one we are serving and the task at hand, the better will we be able to handle both praise and correction rightly; that we are serving something and someone beyond ourselves. As these truths come to live in the mind of the team leader, the leader will find it easier to give encouragement and correction well to team members, and it will be easier for team members to receive what is offered in the right spirit.

A few things to keep in mind concerning the giving of praise and correction:

1. Praise is more important than correction.
This is not to minimize the importance of correction; but it is surprisingly easy to forget to let people know when they have done well, whereas it is easy to spot and give voice to lacks or mistakes. Praise is motivating and inspiriting. If the leader is mainly a faultfinder, those under that leadership will grow discouraged and lose heart for the common effort.

2. Both praise and correction need to be accurate.

It is little help to give general but empty encouragement or general but unspecified correction. Team members need to know where they are doing well and where they should look to improve, and this demands specificity on the part of the leader. False praise or unfair correction is easily spotted and almost always, even if silently, rejected.

3. *Be straightforward, courteous but direct.*

It is important for team members to be confident that if they do well they will be told, and if they do something badly their leader will correct the mistake. This confidence keeps team members from worrying about their performance, or wondering whether there is a negative judgment circulating about them that no one is telling them. Approval or disapproval is best expressed calmly and with specificity. It is a mistake on the leader's part to evoke a vague emotional atmosphere that leaves others with the unpleasant task of deciphering the leader's moods in order to determine how they are doing.

4. *Keep clear the distinction between behavior and being.*

In giving correction, the point is to correct behavior, not to give a judgment about fundamental character. There is a world of difference between saying "You needed, in this instance, to put more energy into the task" and "You are a lazy person." The first allows for improvement and can be energizing; the second will be heard as a blanket condemnation about which it is difficult to know how to respond, and will tend to dispirit the recipient.

5. *Let the feedback be as close to the event as possible.*

A simple but important principle to keep in mind.

⋮ ⋮ ⋮

The leadership skills we have been discussing can be gained or improved by anyone who practices them. But they are not unrelated to deeper matters of character and conviction. Many of the skills enumerated above demand selflessness and self-discipline, and many are based on respect for others. The more a person takes on the character of a true leader, and is growing in habits of putting self aside and serving others, the more easily these skills will be mastered and the more genuinely they will be exercised.

— NOTES —

CHAPTER 12

THE PLACE OF FAILURE IN TRUE LEADERSHIP

Tribulation is a gift from God—one that he especially gives His special friends.
ST. THOMAS MORE

One who makes no mistakes makes nothing.
ST. TERESA OF AVILA

Truly, truly, I say to you, unless a grain of wheat falls into the earth and dies, it remains alone; but if it dies, it bears much fruit.
JOHN 12:24

HERE IS NOTHING particularly profound in the idea that those who aspire to true leadership will need to learn how to deal with failure. It seems a rule of life that we advance through adversity, that nothing of any real significance can be accomplished without perseverance in the face of difficulty. "No pain, no gain" has passed into the language as a truism. Any sensible treatment of the qualities needed for leadership always includes something about the importance of staying the course in dark times, getting up after a fall, remaining courageous in the midst of setback. There is hardly a success story in whatever field of life, from sports, to business, to military campaigns, to love affairs, to losing weight, that doesn't dwell on the significance of pressing on during periods of seeming defeat. We appreciate such stories because they speak to our experience and our deepest instincts. We know that adversity is all around us, and it gives us hope to see examples of triumph in the midst of difficulty. An account of success achieved with nothing but clear sailing would leave us unmoved; we know better than that.

All of this is true and important. But if we are to understand the place of failure in true leadership, we will have to take our considerations to a deeper level. Since true leadership is a mirror of and participation in the leadership of Christ, we need to see how success and failure manifested themselves in his exercise of his leadership. We will then expect a similar pattern to characterize our own.

SUCCESS AND FAILURE IN THE LIFE OF CHRIST

Any examination of the leadership of Christ quickly yields two conclusions that are at first sight difficult to square with one another: first, that Jesus has been among the most successful leaders the world has ever known; and second, that his leadership has often *seemed* to fail.

As to the success of Jesus: there is of course an article of Christian faith here. It stands to reason that if God were to come among the human race, he would accomplish perfectly what he set out to do. This principle is stated by the prophet Isaiah: "For as the rain and the snow come down from heaven, and return not thither but water the earth...so shall my word be that goes forth from my mouth; it shall not return to me empty, but it shall accomplish that which I purpose, and prosper in the thing for which I sent it" (Is 55:11–12). If this is true of every word of God, all the more so is it true of the Incarnate Word. Jesus makes the claim himself at the Last Supper: "While I was with them, I kept them in your name, which you have given me; I have guarded them, and none of them is lost but the son of perdition, that the scripture might be fulfilled" (Jn 17:12). His last words upon the cross, "It is finished," can be understood to mean that all was now accomplished, that he had successfully completed his task. But apart from this principle of faith, there is abundant empirical evidence for the impressive influence of Christ on human history. Over the course of two thousand years he has filled the world with his teaching. His followers number in the billions. His influence has been incalculable in every aspect of human affairs. Whole civilizations have been founded on the faith he came to impart. Even those who want nothing to do with him can hardly deny his enduring significance, and often give testimony to it by the vehemence with which they oppose it. Any reasonable list of the most influential humans who have ever existed would place Jesus of Nazareth very high. Both faith and observation point to the very successful leadership of Christ.

Yet there remains the second truth: that the means by which the influence of Christ upon the world has been gained has often gone under the guise of seeming failure. During the brief time of Christ's public ministry, much of what he attempted apparently went awry. The people of Israel to whom he came with a special mission did not, on the whole, receive him. Their leaders rejected his messianic claim. Many who did follow him had mixed motives, and when things got difficult, went their own way. The project closest to his heart, training a group of disciples whom he came to call his friends and who were to be entrusted with his mission, seemed the worst failure of all. Those disciples regularly misunderstood him and they showed a lamentable slowness to live according to the teaching he gave them. At the climax of his ministry, their leader denied him, another betrayed him, and all but one fled in fear. His messianic task, by all appearances, lay in ruins. Those who saw him crucified could come to only one realistic conclusion: however good an attempt he had made, however well-intentioned he had been, he had failed miserably.

The history of Christ is not the usual story of a person overcoming adversity along the road to glory. It is something more stark and unsettling. In the case of Christ's mission, it looked like failure pure and simple. It was as if Joseph, Jacob's son sold into slavery, had never been given high office in Egypt and had died forgotten in jail; as if Julius Caesar had been killed during the invasion of Gaul and the Roman Empire never founded; as if Thomas Edison had worked day and night and had never managed to invent anything. The strange nature of Christ's triumph was not that he went through hardship and failure in accomplishing his success; it was rather that his failure was, in a mysterious sense, the very root of his success. This is the paradoxical meaning of the Cross: that the cause of Christ is gained by seeming loss; that the very time of defeat is in reality the moment of ringing victory.

SUCCESS AND FAILURE
IN THE HISTORY OF THE CHURCH

The same might be said of the entire history of the Church under Christ's leadership. Taken as a whole, seen in the sweep of its two thousand year course, the Church emerges as the most impressive institution in the history of the world. Its longevity, its universality, its ability to win its way into hearts and minds, its unquenchable spirit that manages to overcome both internal weakness and external enemies, its astonishing vitality that propels it from the wreckage of decayed human cultures to found or inhabit new ones, the glories of its intellectual and spiritual and artistic traditions, the influence of its charitable work—all point to a quality that seems to defy a merely human account of its life. Yet touch any part of that history, look at it in detail, and what do we find? Impressive achievements certainly; but paradoxically a success gained by a constant tale of apparent defeat. The record of Christ's earthly ministry seems forever repeating itself. Christ is received by some, but he is either ignored or rejected by many. He is often treated with violence and humiliation. Among his followers, many are half-hearted, some deny him, some betray him, some co-opt his teaching for their own ends. In the face of all this it can be hard to see how the Church has managed to survive over the centuries at all, let alone grow in influence.

Blessed John Henry Newman once observed this paradoxical characteristic of Christianity:

> Ever since Christianity came into the world, it has been, in one sense, going out of it. It is so uncongenial to the human mind, it is so spiritual, and man is so earthly, it is apparently so defenseless, and has so many strong enemies, so many false friends, that every age, as it comes, may be called "the last time." It has made great conquests, and done great works; but still it has done all, as the Apostle says of himself, "in weakness, and in fear, and in much trembling." *How* it is that it is always failing, yet always continuing, God only knows who wills it,—but so it is; and it is no paradox to say, on the one hand, that it has lasted eighteen hundred years, that it may last many years more, and yet that it draws to an end, nay, is likely to end any day.

THE INTERPRETIVE LENS OF THE CROSS

The success of Christ's leadership amid seeming failure is not accidental: it follows an important principle necessary for any who want to lead truly. Jesus put it this way: "Unless a seed fall to the ground and die, it cannot bear fruit." In the area of successful leadership, things are decidedly not what they seem. Much that is apparently successful is of little importance, and much that seems to be defeat is actually triumph. All of this is both signified and made real by the Cross. The crucifixion of Christ, followed by a dark time in the tomb and then, unlooked-for, a glorious Resurrection, is more than an incalculably important cycle of events; it is the interpretive lens for the whole of life.

If this cruciform pattern is true, then those who attempt to lead truly should expect that their leadership, imitating the pattern of Christ and participating in his life, will follow the lines laid down by him. This means, first, that true leadership holds great promise of success, and those who exercise it should do so with calm confidence. This goes beyond merely hoping that things might go well. It comes with a guarantee: "You did not choose me, but I chose you and appointed you that you should go and bear fruit and that your fruit should abide; so that whatever you ask the Father in my name, he may give it to you" (Jn 15:15). Christ is the pre-eminently successful leader who brings to bear the power and the providence of God in human affairs. There is no rational place for defeatism or discouragement among those who participate in his leadership.

But the cruciform lens also means that we need to gain a new and different understanding of what success looks like in a fallen world, a new way of seeing taught by Christ. We need to master a heavenly language concerning the road the true leader needs to follow, a *via dolorosa* in the footsteps of Christ. Peter underlines this principle in his first letter: "Beloved, do not be surprised at the fiery ordeal which comes upon you to prove you, as though something strange were happening to you. But rejoice in so far as you share Christ's sufferings, that you may also rejoice and be glad when his glory is revealed" (1 Pet 4:12– 13). Peter is not in a "gloom and doom" mode here. His eyes are on the glory and joy that come with triumph. But he knows that the only way to gain that triumph is through a "fiery ordeal." This is so contrary to what we naturally expect that he needs to emphasize the point. "Why are you surprised, why discouraged, why befuddled and perplexed at the stiff opposition you are encountering? Why are you confused that all your efforts seem at the moment to have led nowhere? You act as though this were strange, as though you knew nothing of the cruciform shape of life. Have you forgotten that only what is nailed to the cross and dies can have any share of genuine life? So be filled with joy at the suffering that comes upon you: it is the sign of the kingdom." Those who miss this truth will find themselves distressed and discouraged at the seeming failure of crucifixion and lose hope in the coming success of the resurrection, or, in order to avoid failure, will follow paths of "success" that lead nowhere good or effective.

FAITHFULNESS AND SUCCESS

While failure in this world's terms is a necessary aspect of true success after the cruciform pattern, this does not mean that any and every kind of failure is a sign of the kingdom of God. We need to avoid self-deception. Failure often comes on the heels of incompetence, or laziness, or imprudent decisions, or vicious behavior. There is no room for excusing such failures by claiming that, after all, the Cross comes before the Resurrection. Rather, the point is that we should not be surprised if even our best efforts seem at times to fail, or that we find ourselves unaccountably and powerfully opposed in what we are attempting.

How then do we tell the difference between the failure of the Cross and the failure that comes from human weakness or sin? The main answer is to examine whether we have been acting in fidelity to Christ. When someone once observed to Blessed Mother Teresa that despite her work and the work of her sisters they were still far from successfully eradicating poverty, she famously replied that God had not called her to be successful, but to be faithful. When she said this she was not signing up for failure, or suggesting that her work was really unsuccessful. She was instead redefining the word success, giving it a truer meaning. What might look like "success" for the moment will not be genuine success unless it is accomplished according to the will and plan of God. The road to true success is faithfulness, and what is faithful to God will always succeed. If it sometimes lacks the appearance of success, no surprise; the same was true of the triumphant success of Christ.

PROPER CATEGORIES OF SUCCESS

In the light of this principle, immediate and easily measurable results become less significant. Many of our current categories of success and failure come from the business world. We want metrics that show that sales are improving, new markets are being opened, and the company is growing. According to a business logic, the more such growth the better, provided certain standards of quality and service are maintained. Lack of growth, a turndown, a closing market, diminishing sales, mean that the business is failing. The measurable bottom line becomes the primary definition of success.

Whatever one might say about such an attitude in business, it will not do for evaluating the coming of the Kingdom. True leadership will pay some attention to immediate effects: growth in numbers or lack of growth, a positive or negative reception, a widening or narrowing scope of action, any of which may be signs pointing to areas for necessary improvement or the need to devise new strategies. But the goal of true leadership is not to attain to a particular metric; it is rather to be found faithful to what Christ is doing. One could go so far as to say that for those who participate in Christ's leadership, a consistent and happy growth pattern over time with no serious failure or opposition is an almost sure sign that things are *not* going well. The kingdom of Christ is in necessary conflict with the currents of this world. The forces of darkness are happy to leave alone that which does not threaten their rule. If all is going well all the time, the reason may be that nothing of real significance is being done. Mother Teresa, when establishing a house of her sisters for the first time, would grow uneasy if doors opened too quickly and there seemed to be no problems. Only when she ran into opposition, a roadblock of some kind, an inexplicable practical difficulty, would she grow peaceful, confident that she and her sisters were on the right track. There will be times when our leadership will seem to be successful and others when it will seem to fail. But our ability to know what is happening in the spiritual realm is limited; we are not in a position to see or understand what really makes for success or failure in the broad scheme of things. So our main concern, once prudence and competence have been applied to our best ability, is faithfulness to the one who understands perfectly what is needed, Christ. This is the genuine mark of success.

The lives of the saints show this principle in action. As a group, the saints are the most successful humans who have ever lived. Some of them, though not all, would be viewed as successful even according to this world's standards. But a close look shows a regular pattern: there is always a cruciform shape to their lives and their leadership. Much that they attempt seems to fail, or succeeds only through adversity, or succeeds in measurable ways only after their death. They themselves tend to pay little attention to outward success; their goal is to fashion as true and pure a participation in Christ's life and leadership as they can manage. This was the attitude of that remarkable leader St. Ignatius Loyola. He once said that the only thing that could trouble him would be if the Jesuit order were suppressed by the Pope, which would seem to represent the complete failure of his plans and his leadership. But he went on to say that if after such an occurrence he could spend twenty minutes in prayer meditating on the passion of Christ, he would be just as happy, and even happier, than before. Faithfulness defines success.

THE BATTLE FOR COURAGE

If the Cross is the proper interpretive lens for true leadership, then a key strategic element emerges concerning what it means to be trained in and to exercise genuine leadership: the need to battle for courage. As was noted in an earlier chapter, courage is the determination, leading to a habit and a stance in life, to pursue what is right and good and to keep proper hope alive even when there is a cost involved. It does not mean absence of fear or discomfort in the face of hardship; it is rather the unwillingness to be ruled by what is difficult.

Success in measurable terms encourages us. It brings with it a sense of momentum; it lifts our spirits and makes us feel that what we are doing is important. Even in the midst of hard work and difficult challenges, if things are generally moving forward, growing, expanding, gaining influence, we will not likely face inner discouragement. Quite the opposite: even serious difficulty only makes success sweeter if it comes without too much delay. Speak with members of a championship sports team, or a company that has concluded a successful business venture, and they will dwell with pleasure on the problems along the way, the long hours they put in, and the ingenuity they exercised that finally got them to the top. Their hardships give their triumph its savor.

Seeming failure, on the other hand, discourages us as long as we are operating on a simply natural plane. Hard work, long hours, and careful planning that appear to have little effect, or immediate results that are followed by a long drought and a period of setback; these make our spirits droop, and have us wanting to give the game up. Anyone can stay a course that's going well. But it requires something special to continue to run a road fraught with anxiety, or boredom, or perplexity, or opposition, a road that seems to be getting steeper and narrower and darker with nothing firm to lay hold of. The most common temptation of leaders facing such difficulty is to allow themselves to be caught by creeping discouragement. The word itself shows the process: we become dis-couraged; we lose our courage and are tempted to give up because we do not see the results we had expected.

The proper way to meet the challenge of discouragement is not by calling on heroic stoicism and cultivating an attitude of defiant endurance. "Grinding it out" may have nobility of a kind, but it tends to a brittle and hardened attitude where cynicism and despair, as well as pride, easily find root. What is needed instead is insertion into the mystery of the Crucifixion, an understanding of the true way to gain success and a willingness to participate with Christ as he walks his difficult road toward victory. It is the attitude spoken of repeatedly in the Scriptures, by Jesus and Peter and Paul and James, when they counsel us to rejoice in our sufferings. Why should we be happy about this? Because we like to suffer? Hardly; but because we know that suffering, under the hand of God, brings about all we hope for.

THE ARMOR OF GOD

St. Maximilian Kolbe once noted that all significant accomplishments are based on three pillars: hard work, prayer, and suffering. He was convinced that if any of these were lacking, the project would not go forward successfully. Hard work: yes, we all understand that. And as to prayer we at least give a nod to the need for it, though we may not employ it as much as we should. But the third tends to be off our radar screen entirely. Kolbe is not simply saying that trouble tends to arise and we will have to deal with it. He is looking at success and failure through the interpretive lens of the Cross, and he sees that there will be no success at all, not in the true sense of the word, unless the Cross is involved, which means suffering, which means the temptation to discouragement and the need for courage.

In this matter of failure and success, God has rigged the system. He has promised to those who participate in his life and work that they will succeed, period. His power is greater than that which opposes him, and there is no possibility of ultimate failure for his servants any more than for himself. But there is a condition: we need to stay in the battle. If we fight with the weapons he gives us, eventually we win. So the only way for the enemies of God to stop his plans is to get his servants to lay down their arms. It is therefore no surprise that so much spiritual warfare surrounds this area of courage and discouragement.

In a famous passage from the sixth chapter of the letter to the Ephesians, Paul's main advice for those engaged in fighting the spiritual battle for the Kingdom is to "stand."

Put on the whole armor of God, that you may be able to *stand* against the wiles of the devil. For we are not contending against flesh and blood, but against the principalities, against the powers, against the world rulers of this present darkness, against the spiritual hosts of wickedness in the heavenly places. Therefore take the whole armor of God, that you may be able to with*stand* in the evil day, and having done all, to *stand*. *Stand* therefore. (Eph 6:11–13, author emphasis)

It is an interesting encouragement for those going into battle. Paul, one of history's greatest leaders, marshals his troops and readies them for conflict. In words filled with fervor and high confidence, he tells them, not "Charge!" not "Attack!" not "Go get 'em!" but "Stand." It seems something of an anticlimax. "Don't run away" is good basic advice for a soldier, but hardly what we expect to hear in an inspirational pep talk. But Paul knows that the fiercest battle rages exactly around this posture. Those who stand where Christ has placed them and serve him faithfully will succeed, even in the face of seeming defeat, as long as they keep fighting; as long as they remember that true leadership follows the cruciform pattern of their Master; as long as they do not give up.

The Place of Failure in Leadership

— NOTES —

PART III

The Nature and Purpose of Institutions

CHAPTER 13

WHY INSTITUTIONS?

*Behold, I have taught you statutes and ordinances, as the Lord my God
commanded me. Keep them and do that; for that will be your wisdom
and your understanding in the sight of the peoples.... For what great
nation is there, that has statutes and ordinances so righteous as all this
law which I set before you this day?*

DEUTERONOMY 4:5–6; 8

IN OUR DEFINITION of true leadership we noted that leadership usually takes place in the context of common institutional life. Here we are
taking up that question in more detail. What then is an institution, and
why are institutions important? This is a vital aspect of proper leadership.

Angels need no institutions. They do not inhabit time or space; their
life is in the unfathomable eternal now of the presence of God. Their
knowledge of God, of truth, of themselves, is immediate and constant.
They are immaterial. They need no traditions, no forms for living. They
reflect in unending joy and wonder the infinite being of God.

Irrational animals need no institutions. They have no sense of time
or of eternity. They do not wonder about what lies behind the physical
world, or what will happen at the end of their lives. They live by what

we call instinct, by an immediate response to their physical environment. They are provided by nature with what they need to survive, and they live without forethought and without judgment.

Humans are hybrids. We are made of the same material stuff as irrational animals, and we inhabit the same physical world. Materially speaking we are bound like them to the possibilities and limitations of time and space. Nonetheless, we have access to the eternal, to ideals of truth, beauty, and goodness, to the being of God. The past and the future are present to us. "He has made everything beautiful in its time; also he has put eternity into man's mind" (Ecc 3:11). This tension is the backdrop to the drama of the human race: we are time-bound creatures who long for eternity, material beings graced with immortal souls, who live in the present moment and in an immediate physical environment but who are oriented to times and to places that transcend our circumstances, and ultimately to the bursting of the bonds of time and space.

Unlike the angels, whose choice in serving or not serving God was immediate, and unlike the animals, whose destiny is unknown to us but is not determined by their own choice, humans have been placed on what Aquinas called the "slow way" to the Kingdom of God. We are pilgrims, wanderers, journeying to our true home, day by day making the decisions that will ultimately determine our destiny.

Because of our created nature as temporal and spatial beings, humans by necessity and without exception live in institutions. This term, institution, is used in different ways, and often has a somewhat stodgy feel to it. Here is what we mean by it: "An institution is a form, a pattern, a nexus of practical life and ordered relationship, made concrete and held together by a combination of law, custom, practices, art and architecture, words, anything that comes of the stuff of the created world, within which and through which our ideas, our ideals, our understanding of our world and ourselves, and our hopes for eternity, can be incarnated, sustained, grow, and come to fruition through time."

INSTITUTIONS AND THE DIVINE PLAN

If our ideals and our relationships are not incarnated, that is, not formed into institutions, they will sooner or later be lost to us. Usually sooner. When God created Adam and Eve, his intention for them was that they would live in a union of love with himself and with each other, that they would be fruitful and have children, and they would order the world to goodness and beauty. It is recorded that Adam was delighted with Eve; they evidently loved each other. But without a stable form of life there was no possibility of love's survival against the forgetfulness and ravages of time. So God provided that as well. "Therefore a man leaves his father and his mother and cleaves to his wife and they become one flesh" (Gen 2:24). Marriage is the final touch of God's creation, the institutional matrix within which humanity comes into its true being, without which it remains vulnerable, stunted, and unfulfilled.

When God acted to save the human race after our fall from goodness, he gathered a people to himself and gave them a form of life within which they could maintain their ideals and their identity. He established a code of justice, a priesthood, a set of holy days and seasons, a place and a way of worship, and a hierarchy of administrative order by means of which he could dwell with them. This way of life involving statute and custom and relationship was called by the Israelites "the Law." They were to keep the Law carefully "that your days may be prolonged, that it may go well with you, and that you may multiply greatly in a land flowing with milk and honey" (Deut 6:2–3). It was the institutional context that would allow the Chosen People to flourish and prosper. It was also laid down that these forms were to be passed on from generation to generation: "You shall teach them diligently to your children, and shall talk of them when you sit in your house, and when you walk by the way, and when you lie down, and when you rise" (Deut 6:7). The Jewish people understood this ordering of space and time by the hand of God to be their greatest blessing, their pride, and their consolation. "The law of the Lord is perfect, reviving the soul; the precepts of the Lord are right, rejoicing the heart. More to be desired are they than gold, even much fine gold; sweeter also than honey and drippings of the honeycomb" (Ps 19:7,11).

When God re-created the human race in Christ, he likewise established an institution in which the renewed call to love of God and neighbor could be realized and could take true form. Though Jesus wrote no books, conquered no empires, and erected no monuments, he was still pre-eminently a builder. He left behind him the Church, an ordered institution that he then informed and inhabited by his Holy Spirit, which would become the true home of the human race. His words to Peter, "On this rock I will build my Church, and the powers of death will not prevail against it" (Mt 16:18) show how important the establishment of the Church was for the accomplishment of his plans. When the third century bishop Cyprian of Carthage wrote, "You cannot have God for your father unless you have the Church for your mother," he was pointing to the necessity of this divinely ordained institution for the fulfillment of the plan of God in Christ.

God created the human race to live in an institutional framework. This means that to be anti-institutional is at some level to be anti-human. Institutions are a good and necessary part of the created order. The point is to keep them strong and healthy.

PRIMARY, SECONDARY, AND TERTIARY INSTITUTIONS

Human society is an interlocking network of different kinds of institutions. There are important distinctions to make among them, distinctions that are here highlighted by placing them into three groupings (primary, secondary, and tertiary) according to the centrality of their importance to human life and meaning. These different types of institutions are intertwined, often embedded within one another, related to each other in ways that make a neat separation between them impossible. Nonetheless the distinctions are important. We might think of them as a series of concentric circles, the most important at the center, the others radiating outward but still connected to and in some sense dependent upon and giving depth to the central ones.

Primary Institutions

There are two institutions that are founded and given form through the direct action of God. They are the family and the Church. These are our *primary* institutions, the most important ones within which we live. It is in these institutions alone that we are meant to find fundamental meaning. They are our primary place of belonging and of loyalty. Each is secured by sacramental grace, guaranteeing God's presence and purpose in them. These two institutions are related to each other and are meant to complement and support one another.

At the very heart of our life and meaning, the institution that is before all others and will outlast all others is the Church. The Church is our true home, the place we find our true selves, both temporally and eternally, the place of the dwelling of God himself. The Church unites earth and heaven, angels and humanity, past, present, and future, in an order of beauty and truth. This is why the claims of the Church are ultimate ones. Only in the Church do we find the whole of our being, physical and spiritual, temporal and eternal, addressed and cared for and brought to fulfillment. Jesus makes clear that even visà-vis family, which is a kind of shadow of the Church, there are times when obligations to the Church take precedence (cf. Mt 10:35–37). Nonetheless these two institutions—family and Church—are not opposed to each other. The family is meant to be the "domestic Church," the first teacher of the faith, the foundational form of the Church's love and worship. And the Church calls herself a family, one whose Father is God. Mary is the Blessed Mother; the Pope is named the Holy Father; priests are addressed as fathers; Church members call one another brother and sister. Believers recognize in each other their true family. "Whoever does the will of my Father is my brother and sister and mother" (Mk 3:35).

These two primary institutions, Church and family, are of such importance that God not only brought them into existence, but he also gave them their definitive form, one that was not fundamentally to be altered. The sacrament of marriage was established by God as a lifelong bond between a man and a woman oriented to unity and fruitfulness as a share in the union and creative action of the Trinity. Christ asserted its divine origin and its indissolubility by the command, "What God has joined together, let not man put asunder" (Mt 19:6). Likewise, the Church, called by Paul "the pillar and ground of truth" (1 Tim 3:15), was explicitly founded by Christ upon the rock of Peter and on the foundation stones of the apostles, with an organization, a way of worship, and a code of behavior laid down by him. Those who attempt to rewrite the structure of the family or to rework the form of the Church set themselves at odds with the stated plan of God, and put the welfare of humanity at risk. At the very least they lay themselves and others open to deformity, since it is these two institutions, when properly constituted, which allow us to grow fully into our humanity.

In the Jewish-Christian tradition, to "keep holy the Lord's Day" is the command that has enjoined the maintenance of the divinely sanctioned human order as expressed in these two primary institutions. For the Jews, the Sabbath Day, one day out of every seven, was given especially to the worship of God in Temple or Synagogue, and to spending time with family. It was a day set apart to re-create and re-order the world after a week of the creeping disorders of time and space, to revitalize human life, to refocus the gaze of the heart upon God, the ultimate source of meaning. One can see the power of such a practice in the history of the Jewish people, who though scattered across the world have for millennia been able to maintain their ideals, their vision of God and way of life, because those ideals were enshrined in the institutional stuff of their lives, the anchor of which was the keeping of the Sabbath. Christians continued this practice and brought it a new universality by their observance of Sunday as the Day of the Resurrection. We need not look far to see the loss of meaning and concomitant chaotic despair that settles upon those who become detached from keeping the Day of the Lord and so lose their proper integration in these two life-giving institutions.

True leadership begins and finds its most important expression in the leadership of the primary institutions of family and Church. Not only are they the most important for the sake of proper human flourishing, they are also the training ground for other forms of leadership. They provide the template for secondary and tertiary institutions. A just social order begins with acknowledging the essential importance of family life, and a just government honors properly the freedom of the Church.

Secondary Institutions

Apart from the primary institutions of family and Church, two other kinds of institutions, broadly speaking, can be identified. First among them are those institutions that are ordained and supported by God as natural and necessary for human life, but whose specific form has been left to humans to sort out according to custom, prudence, and just principles. These are *secondary* institutions. The most obvious of these are four: governmental institutions that deal with political life, economic institutions that order the workings of the market, educational institutions that train the young, and charitable institutions for the care for those in need.

As to *governmental institutions*: Jesus's words "Give to Caesar what is Caesar's" (Mt 22:21) and Peter's exhortation "Honor the emperor" (1 Pet 2:17) express the importance of these institutions. God creates humans as social beings, and social life by its nature demands governance. In this sense, human government is upheld by God, since it is implicit in the created order. The Roman Empire that Jesus and Peter here refer to was not the only conceivable form of government; other governmental forms might be, and have been, developed. America is a democracy; medieval France was a monarchy; Venice was for a thousand years an oligarchy. But some form of government is necessary for a just and reasonable social order. It is a serious human task to maintain governmental arrangements as much as possible according to the dictates of reason and justice, the principles of which are often enshrined in custom and tradition.

As to *economic institutions*: because we live in a world of matter and time, a flourishing common life demands material support, which requires a certain division of labor and a just distribution of the goods of the world. "Now such persons we command and exhort in the Lord Jesus Christ to do their work in quietness and to earn their own living" (2 Thes 3:12). Proper work demands a context: the farm, the shop, the business, the apparatus of trade, of buying and selling. There will necessarily be institutional forms of economic life under which a just handling of material goods can take place. Most people spend most of their lives in such institutions, so their proper establishment and care is of great practical importance.

As to *educational institutions*: the Proverb says: "Discipline your son while there is hope; do not set your heart on his destruction" (Prov 19:18). Because children come into the world without what they need to survive and flourish, education is necessary to human life. Education of children has always been understood by Christians as a divinely given duty, performed in many ways and under many institutional forms. Much education takes place in home and family, but Christians and Jews, and all human societies, have constructed educational institutions of various kinds to help in accomplishing this necessary task. We call our schools Alma Mater, our dear mother, and speak of teachers as acting *in loco parentis*, in the parents' stead. A primary institution, in this case the family, provides the inner form of a secondary one, the school.

As to *charitable institutions*: it is a by-product of a fallen world that there will inevitably be sickness, poverty, the elderly and infirm, orphaned children, people who have suffered from the ravages of war or from natural disasters or of ill-treatment at the hands of others. Caring for those in need, and finding institutional forms for that care, is a necessary task. Traditionally such institutions—hospitals, orphanages, homes for the aged, organizations for feeding the poor or helping refugees—were rooted in the Church and the family. The Church has been the most extensive charitable organization the world has known, and Christians of all kinds have founded and run many charitable works. More recently, governments have taken on a great deal of charitable work, and many non-governmental private institutions have been founded as well.

Secondary institutions demand attention and prudent thought. Because they are necessary, even divinely ordained by the order of creation, all humans will live under some form of them. But such forms are often corrupt, or unjust, or seriously inadequate. This is why Christians (among others) have spent so much energy in articulating sound principles for the maintenance of political, economic, educational, and charitable institutions. An important aspect of this articulation is to rightly understand the relationship of such institutions to the primary ones of family and Church. Such concerns are highly controverted and important issues in our own time: Church and state questions, issues surrounding educational institutions and the family, and adjusting the claims of the corporate world and family life.

Tertiary Institutions

Finally there are institutions of many kinds, here called *tertiary*, which are established for specific and limited reasons in order to accomplish particular ends. Examples would include an army corps, an academy of arts, a sports team, a news service, and a bridge club. Also included would be specific economic, educational, charitable, or governmental institutions: an individual business, a particular school, a hospital. Such institutions are often important in themselves, and taken together they make up much of the fabric of civil society. They are usually related in an organic way to primary and secondary institutions and are engaged in the purposes of those institutions; to that degree they are particular or partial instantiations of them. Tertiary institutions are conceived in creativity and prudent thought, endure for a longer or shorter time, and are under the authority of those who establish and look after them.

Humans have always had an instinct for the importance of institutions, a kind of sense for civilization, and have made heroes of those who founded or protected their civilization's leading institutions. Moses and the giving of the Jewish Law, Hammurabi and the code of the Babylonians, Solon and the political ordering of Athens, Plato and his Academy, Aeneas and his protection of his father and family amid the wreckage of Troy and the founding of Rome, Confucius and the practices of the *Li*, St. Benedict and the establishing of Western monasticism, the American Founders at the Constitutional Congress: all were builders or protectors of institutions. We have a natural admiration for those who have founded a school or a hospital or a business, or for the person who planted a mission church or opened an orphanage or first brought land under the plow. We understand that they have done something important that deserves gratitude. A civilization is a complex interconnection of various institutional forms, gathered around a cohering ideal, a spiritual vision that historically has almost always been a religion. A healthy and growing civilization is one that has the energy and ability to authentically institutionalize its ideals. A decaying or corrupted civilization is one that has forgotten the importance of institutions or has lost the ability to found and sustain healthy institutions.

What then does it mean for an institution to be healthy? That is the topic for the next chapter.

— NOTES —

CHAPTER 14

≈   ≈

KEEPING INSTITUTIONS HEALTHY

Woe to you, scribes and Pharisees, hypocrites! for you tithe mint and dill and cumin, and have neglected the weightier matters of the law, justice and mercy and faith; these you ought to have done, without neglecting the others.

MATTHEW 23:23

PUTTING FIRST THINGS FIRST

The primary institutions of family and Church are the proper location for our deepest sense of belonging and loyalty. But it is also true that institutions of whatever kind, when healthy, whether of government or business or education, or even entertainment, attempt to keep in view and to ground themselves in the principles of the two primary institutions, while being careful not to replace them. Such principles include the following:

* The fundamental dignity and eternal destiny of all humans;

● The priority of our moral and spiritual nature over our material concerns;

● The priority of human relationship over utility;

● The imperative to protect the weakest members;

● Concern for the common good of all.

These principles are applied differently in different institutions, but any institution, however limited, that neglects them will exact a human and spiritual price from its members.

The Church and the family, founded as they are by God himself, come first. They do not gain their legitimacy from other institutions. It is rather the duty of other institutions to recognize their priority, to give them encouragement, and to help them to flourish, at the very least to allow them adequate room for their proper functioning. A government, a business, or a school, while legitimately pursuing a good purpose, needs to be constituted such that it does not harm or destroy Church or family. To do so would be to infringe upon a basic human right. When parents insist on raising and educating their children according to their own best lights, or when the Church presses for freedom to practice the faith in peace, they are pointing to the prior right of family and Church in these matters, and calling the civil authorities properly to honor that right.

We live in a time of increasing, and increasingly unjust, challenges to the existence of our two primary institutions. A typical form of this challenge occurs when secondary institutions attempt to replace primary institutions by usurping their role and setting themselves up as the source of basic meaning and identity. Secondary institutions, necessary and useful as they are, need to honor their proper bounds. First things first, second things second.

The temptation to put second things first is particularly evident in the realm of politics. It is a dangerous tendency of our age, stemming from secular Enlightenment thought, to treat the state, understood as a political entity, as *the* primary institution of the society. We are given to believe that the state is the place of ultimate meaning, the human thing to which we most truly belong. Politicians and political programs are then looked to not as aids to public good but as sources of personal fulfillment and integration. Under this scheme, the political state claims to meet all the needs, physical and spiritual, of its members, to be the context in which all human problems will be solved. As a result it feels itself free to make absolute claims on those under its authority. It assumes to itself roles that it has neither the right nor the capacity to fulfill. This has expressed itself most dreadfully in recent history in the imposition of totalitarian statist ideologies. Those in the political realm who have embraced the view that the state is primary, in whatever form it arises, will tend to look with jealousy at all other institutions not under their control, especially those that claim priority and insist on performing their role of safeguarding human identity. Political institutions captured by this kind of thinking will sooner or later attack both the family and independent religious bodies specifically as institutions. They may allow private and individual expressions of faith and of human affection, but they will attempt to dominate or destroy anything outside of the state that possesses institutional weight.

One sees the propensity to put second things first also in the world of economics, in the workings of the market. When humans are seen not as immortal beings with inherent dignity, but merely as producers and consumers to be fitted into market economics, all manner of human degradation occurs. The concern for the just distribution of goods and the right of private property, an important if secondary thing, is claimed as the primary thing, the highest good for humans. If only we become wealthy, we will be happy and our deepest desires will be fulfilled. All is then subordinated to maximizing wealth, or, conversely, to equalizing it. Human success is seen in strictly economic terms, and poverty is deemed the worst of human ills. We do not need to look far to see examples of the rampant greed, the enslaving work, and the profound harm to human dignity and worth that such an orientation produces, whether its practitioners are on the "right" or the "left" of the economic spectrum. At best this reduction of the human to our material needs tends to make us small-souled, content with the baubles and trinkets of a passing age rather than embracing the true nobility of our nature.

Any secondary or tertiary institution can fall into this trap of putting second things first: the school that attempts to replace the family by monopolizing the time and energies of its students, the sports team that eats into both family and Church life, the workplace that demands excessive hours and that commands a loyalty that puts primary concerns at risk. Because secondary institutions, while important and necessary, are miserably bad at being primary institutions, in part because they are not equipped to deal with the eternal human soul, the result of this usurpation by secondary institutions is profound wounds to the human spirit. Fending off such challenges and properly adjusting the claims of primary with other human institutions is one of the main civilizational challenges of our time. Much will depend on how we meet it.

FAILURES CONCERNING INSTITUTIONS

Given the necessity of institutions for the proper development of humanity, there can arise three main temptations leading to failures in regard to them. These are: (1) to rely on the form of an institution but to neglect its founding ideals and its necessary spirit; (2) to understand the need for institutions, but to build them badly, inhumanly; and (3) to seek freedom from institutions altogether.

The First Temptation: Form Without Spirit
Every married couple knows the lurking possibility of this failure. They

marry because they love each other and want their lives intertwined. They find joy and goodness in the prospect of a shared future. The institution of marriage is designed to aid that ideal and that desire, to secure it and allow it to come to fruition. Marriage gives a public existence to their relationship with privileges and duties attached. Civil law acknowledges special rights as well as necessary duties of spouses. Family and friends look upon the marriage as a settled relationship and welcome the couple into their lives as a unity. Other potential mates recognize the permanence of the marriage bond and leave it in peace. A shared household gives the relationship spatial stability and a place for the raising of children. Laws of inheritance allow for the continuity of the family's life over the years. All of this aids the love that animates the married couple and their family. But these institutional forms, though good, cannot be a replacement for the ideals at its core. The institution of marriage is a road upon which to travel, a home within which to live. It exists to be used, to provide the means and the occasion for the life and growth of the loving ideal at its heart. If once the spirit is lost, if once love grows cold, the lifeless form becomes an irritation and a burden. This was Jesus's concern with the Pharisees in their spiritual leadership of the Jewish people. "Woe to you, scribes and Pharisees, hypocrites! for you tithe mint and dill and cumin, and have neglected the weightier matters of the law, justice and mercy and faith; these you ought to have done, without neglecting the others" (Mt 23:23). Without neglecting the others: Jesus does not criticize the Pharisees for paying attention to institutional matters, in this case the law concerning tithing. Rather, he takes the Pharisees to task for having lost the point of the institution as a whole, justice and mercy and faith; for following the letter of the law but not the spirit.

An unfortunate and unhistorical picture of Jesus has gained currency that portrays him as an iconoclastic rebel pitted against the very existence of the institutions of his day. According this view, institutional forms by their nature spell death to spiritual ideals, and an institutionalized religion is a lifeless one. Jesus thus came to destroy the forms of religion in order to leave behind a spiritual and non-institutional faith. This misreads both the scriptural and historical picture of Jesus and the early Church entirely. In fact, Jesus was not in the least anti-institutional. He worked not to destroy, but to reform and fulfill existing institutions.

The letter kills and the Spirit gives life (2 Cor 3:6). The Spirit animates the letter, so that it is not a lifeless, but rather a life-giving form. Jesus himself insists that he came "not to abolish the law but to fulfill it" (Mt 5:17), in particular to fill out and more firmly establish the two most important institutions of Church and family. So, for example, the Jews honored marriage but allowed divorce; Jesus insisted that marriage was of such importance in the original plan of God that it was indissoluble. The Jews understood themselves as the Chosen People ordered religiously and politically under God; Jesus extended the understanding of the Chosen to all who believed in the Messiah, and distinguished between the primary institution of the Church and the secondary one of the state. The Jews ordered themselves under twelve tribes, descendants of the sons of Jacob; Jesus chose and trained twelve apostles and gave them and those they ordained after them office and authority in the Church. The Jews celebrated the rite of Passover; Jesus fulfilled that celebration in the institution of the Eucharist. The Jews had an order of worship, a priesthood, and various rites of purification; Jesus taught a fulfilled form of worship, established a new priesthood, and instituted the rite of baptism as a means of inward renewal of life. In all of this Jesus was concerned to rightly establish and give proper form to primary institutions, and to fill those forms with the Holy Spirit, the "Lord and giver of life." It is no accident that the Church has been the most impressively fruitful institution in human history. It has taken after its Founder and is animated by his Spirit.

The same principle of form and spirit is at work in other institutions as well. A business that loses its focus will founder and go under. A political party whose ideals become incoherent or corrupt will leak membership and fall from power or will harm those under its governance. A sports team that loses its spirit will get soundly beaten. This principle explains the proliferation of vision statements and party planks and slogans; why married couples go on retreats to remember and renew their love; why religious orders meditate on the charisms of their founders; why businesses hold vision days for their members. The Church understands herself as constantly returning to her inner spirit. She doesn't change her fundamental institutional form, which is given her by God in Christ. Rather, she recasts what has become corrupted, she attends to her true shape, and she refills that institutional form with the life and love at its heart. A body needs its various systems—skeletal and muscular and nervous—for its proper functioning, but without a living soul it is still nothing but a corpse.

The Second Temptation: Building Unhealthy Institutions

To generalize a phrase from the teaching of Jesus: institutions were made for man, not man for institutions. Jesus said this concerning the Sabbath, but the same could be said of any institution. Much of the problem of finding ourselves in institutional arrangements that deform our humanity arises from their faulty construction. It works this way: a modicum of thought will lead to the conclusion that institutions of some kind are necessary to get much of anything accomplished in life. So we construct them, we endure them, and we put a certain energy into their maintenance. But if we stop thinking at that point, the institutions we build or maintain will easily become corrupted and unhealthy. If we view institutions from a simply utilitarian point of view, as instrumental means to accomplish a goal and nothing more, we will find that we have created or allowed to develop an institutional wasteland where the air is too thin to breathe.

A cardinal principle for any healthy institution is the primacy of the human. Our institutions, of whatever kind, need to have a human scale; they need to begin with the concern that they will not impede, but rather aid the humanity of those involved. Whatever other legitimate goals they may have, whether making money, or keeping social order, or winning ball games, or turning out well-trained workers, or pursuing physical and mental health, or selling products, or advancing science, they need to pursue those goals in such a way as to further the genuinely human quality of those they touch.

In this, the institutions of family and of Church have a role to play as a kind of template for other institutions. A family may have—and in many societies does have—many different ends. It is often an economic unit; it is sometimes a political unit; it is always a place of education, often a place for the giving of care to the sick and the elderly, a local center of the arts and of other cultural expressions, a hub of social life, a center of religious worship and teaching, and a focal point for relationships of love and commitment. These varied activities involve many different roles, but in a (healthy) family none of these activities are pursued apart from attentiveness to the overall good of the individuals involved. Children might work on the family farm or in the family restaurant, but they are not driven as slaves to the detriment of their health; the sick and weak are cared for as individuals who are known and loved; the young are educated by people who care about them; the overall prosperity of the family is not achieved through the destruction of its members. This is one reason why the family is the great humanizing institution. It is the primary place where we develop our true selves in relation to others and to the common good in the midst of various activities.

Likewise, the Church is a multi-faceted institution that worships, educates, serves the needy, catechizes, and involves itself in various contemporary social issues. It has a structure of government, a body of teaching, a judicial system, and a set of customs and rites. It owns land; it runs churches and schools, hospitals and orphanages, cultural centers, cemeteries, and a hundred other organizations and initiatives. It has an economic aspect, a political aspect, and an intellectual aspect. But in all these activities, when it is doing its job properly, it is something more than merely a center of activity: it is a home for its members, a school of humanity. Its primary goal is the good of those with whom it is in various ways connected, whatever other secondary goals it has in view. Thus the Church is concerned for the poor and the sick as individual immortal beings, and will not let impatience with poverty or disease lead to remedies that dehumanize or eradicate those they are meant to serve. The Church is concerned for the academic excellence of its members, but not at the risk of damaging their consciences or their souls. The Church favors scientific advance, but not if the advance is really a retreat, and tends to the enslavement or destruction of humans. The Church honors the good of economic prosperity, but not to the point of placing temporary wealth ahead of eternal happiness, or of using humans in inhuman ways to make money.

Other human institutions have more limited goals than family and Church, and need to be aware of those limits. But in their measure and according to their purposes, they will be healthy to the degree that they assume the same underlying principles. They will become unhealthy, corrupt, and dehumanizing to the degree that they forget them or set them aside. Human scale is primary.

UNHEALTHY INSTITUTIONS AND SOCIAL ENGINEERING. There is another form of unhealthy institutions common in our current society. It arises from the attitude that recognizes the importance of institutions, but exaggerates that importance to the peril of our fundamental freedom. According to this view, institutions do not merely provide the proper home for the truly human to emerge: they entirely shape the nature of the humans under their influence. If one wants a certain type of person, then one builds a certain kind of institution, and like hot wax under a mold the human will be shaped by the institutional form. This way of thinking has its roots in certain of the educational philosophers of the Enlightenment, noteworthy among them Rousseau, who insisted that evil in the world came to us externally, from bad institutions. Again, the thought of Condorcet is helpful: "Is there any vicious habit, any practice contrary to good faith, any crime, whose origin and first cause cannot be traced back to the legislation, the institutions, the prejudices of the country wherein this habit, this practice, this crime can be observed?" In order to remedy human evil, one simply needs to construct good institutions. Humans are so much raw material to be squeezed, smelted, shaped, and ultimately manipulated by institutional structures. There is a truth in this view; institutions are important, and do seriously affect those under their influence. But institutions are not all-powerful, and human nature is not all-malleable. Humans are not laboratory rats: we cannot construct institutions that do away with human evil by denying human freedom. The dominance of this utopian attitude has given rise to the pervasive and pestilential breed of social engineers, that numerous class who create never-ending laws and procedures and regulations, thinking thereby to recreate and perfect the human race. Karl Marx was a proponent of this way of thinking, and his twentieth-century disciple Antonio Gramsci, the father of modern socialism, developed the idea of cultural hegemony as the way to transform society and to eradicate its evil, a process famously characterized by his followers as "the long march through institutions." Of such people the poet T. S. Eliot once wrote, "They constantly try to escape from the darkness outside and within by dreaming of systems so perfect that no one will need to be good." In a world under the influence of such a vision, personal responsibility gets lost and with it human freedom, and institutions tend to a rampant growth of enslaving and dehumanizing bureaucratic forms.

The Third Temptation: Desiring to be Free of Institutional Limitations Entirely

When an institution loses its founding ideals and its action becomes dry and lifeless, those under its influence experience it as heavy and irksome. At this point another temptation arises: that of thinking that the problem is with the very existence of the institution itself. This attitude is common in our day. We live amid a strong current of anti-institutionalism.

There are various sources of this prevalent anti-institutional attitude. One source we already touched upon: the rejection of long-standing traditions and the pursuit of rationally generated utopian visions. A common expression of this understanding champions what has been called the "imperial self." We will find the greatest measure of human freedom and the best chance to live good and happy lives, not by being rightly related to healthy institutions such as family and Church, which would mean paying attention to tradition and custom and long-standing arrangements, but by breaking free from all institutional restraints to pursue individual desires and goals. Marriage is thus seen as a form of slavery, children as a limitation, and family authority as overbearing. The Church is viewed as an oppressive force that gets in the way of individual freedom and authenticity. All authority of whatever kind is by nature suspect, traditions are discredited as being "out of date," and autonomous choice becomes all-important. The sixties of the last century saw an efflorescence of this kind of self-oriented utopian experimentation. We see expressions of this attitude everywhere: bumper stickers that proclaim "Question Authority," calls for sexual liberation in the pursuit of personal erotic fulfillment, attempts to "free" individuals from the constraints of gender. The sentiment "I'm into spirituality, but I'm against organized religion" moves in a similar direction.

Ultimately this attitude is rooted in the desire to escape the inevitable limits of creaturehood, and to live as though time and space did not matter. There is a familiar story line of sentimental but unrealistic lovers who chafe against what they see as the constraints of marriage. "Our love is enough for us," they insist. "We don't need a piece of paper to prove it; we won't love each other more because we tie ourselves to a social convention. Worse, it would lessen our love, because it would make it seem weak and in need of external support." If such lovers were angels, their thinking would be reasonable enough. But being humans they are only trying to evade the possibilities and limitations of the "slow way." The immediate experience of the love of the moment is not enough, is never enough, not because it is not intense enough or rich enough or selfless enough at that particular instant, but because without a settled and ordered form, without an institution, it hasn't the capacity to survive the changes of time and circumstance or to grow into its fullest expression. An outdoor family picnic on a warm summer afternoon may be a delightful experience; but despite the fruit on the trees and the splashing of the water in the brook and the delicate breeze, it isn't enough for the sustenance of family life. When cold and rain and sickness and lack of food make their inevitable arrival, when time and change impinge, the picnickers will need a house to live in if they are not to perish. As the homeless are to a settled human life—lost and vulnerable and often barely surviving—so are ideals without institutions. We cannot escape our creatureliness, and there is no happiness in attempting it. If we try, we will find we are chasing a dream, and will end up facing a desolating homelessness of soul, wandering from our true dignity and purpose.

THE COWBOY IDEAL

Yet another aspect of our aversion to institutions is expressed in our love affair with the cowboy. The cowboy is the great American hero: he shows up not only in westerns, but in different guise in cop shows and space adventures and action films of all kinds. There is much to admire in the typical cowboy: courage, endurance, readiness to act, skill of various kinds. The classic scene is played out in a hundred ways. We're in a frontier setting, and there is good land and endless possibilities for the settlers, but bad things are afoot. A corrupt rancher has bought off the sheriff and hired a gang of hooligans and is running a personal regime of rapacity and violence. Good folk are getting hurt, fear is running high, and no one seems able to stop it. Then into town rides a tall silent stranger. No one knows where he came from. He enters the saloon with a slow stride, and a hush settles over the room. After a few tense run-ins with the bad guys, he gets flinty-eyed and determined. By a combination of grit, savvy, skill with guns and fists, and a measure of good luck, he runs the ruffians out of town, does away with the corrupt sheriff, and puts the good guys back on their feet. He breaks the paralysis of the townspeople with decisive action. The mayor is grateful, and the local beauty has stars in her eyes, hoping the stranger might settle down and call the town his home. But he doesn't linger. He has other horizons in his gaze. They all watch quietly as he mounts his horse and rides off slowly into the sunset.

It's an attractive story line. The difficulty is that very few problems in life are solved in this fashion, nor can they be. The cowboy mentality reveals a lack of understanding of the true nature of human life as embedded in institutions, a lack that is not surprising in a society like ours that so prizes the individual. Courage, bravery, and readiness to act are excellent qualities; but if they are not translated into determined, intelligent, and patient efforts to establish sound and lasting institutions or to reform corrupt ones, they will have little ultimate effect. Those who take the cowboy approach may look impressive for the moment, but they do not change much around them. They might in fact do a good deal of harm.

BUREAUCRACY AND INSTITUTIONS

Still another understandable source of our modern anti-institutional attitude is our difficult experience with the institutions we inhabit. We face a technological and bureaucratic social order dominated by the machine that has deformed and dehumanized our institutions. Our schools often look and feel like prisons, our offices are mazes of cubicles and garish lights, our time and our relationships are measured and mechanized in unnatural ways. What's to wonder that we seek a way out, a vacation from the "rat race," a free weekend to "kick back and be ourselves." Having constructed unlivable institutional environments, we find that we need to escape them to a refuge where we can recover. The desire to get back to nature, the sentiment "I don't want to feel like a number," the love of informality, the recognition of stress as a constant companion, are in part responses to this uneasy and understandable sense of deformation.

The important principle to remember is that we all live in institutional arrangements. Even those who say they don't, do. It is a simple necessity for anything that lasts beyond the moment, whether political, or religious, or economic, or relational. Ideas, ideals, relationships, all seek institutional forms by a law of their nature. Those who think they can do away with institutions never succeed in doing so. They only subject themselves (and others) to arbitrary and often hidden institutional arrangements that do not reflect the accumulated wisdom of time or the work of careful thought, and so prove tyrannous or corrupting. The question is not, will we live institutionally? The question is rather, will we live in healthy institutions that make us more truly human, or will we live in unhealthy institutions that deform our humanity?

In facing unhealthy, deformed, or corrupt institutions, of which there are many, the task then becomes, not to escape them, but to repair them, or if necessary to build new ones. The right response to a leaky roof is to fix it or to find a new home, not to do away with houses. The proper solution to poison is to prepare healthy food, not to stop eating altogether.

THE NEED FOR INSTITUTIONAL LEADERSHIP

What does all this talk about institutions have to do with leadership? A great deal. If institutions are the matrix within which we live, if healthy institutions are among the great gifts we possess and are important for our proper human and spiritual maturity, if unhealthy institutions deform and corrupt us, then it becomes vital that we understand institutions and learn how to lead them well. Leadership largely takes place in the context of institutional life. A good and effective leader will understand the nature and the purpose of institutions and will know how to keep them healthy; a bad or ineffective leader will not.

The typical denizen of the modern world has little understanding of the importance of institutions, or of how to maintain them and purify them, which is to say, little sense of civilization. This is the real meaning of barbarism, and, despite our technological brilliance, we live in an increasingly barbaric age. A great need of our time as regards leadership is to regain an understanding of institutions, and to take up the task of leading them well. This task will involve, among other things:

* Understanding the importance of institutions for the proper flourishing of human life;

* Identifying principles of institutional life, oriented to a human scale, that come from primary institutions;

* Understanding how to purify or re-form institutions that have become corrupt and notably, appreciating the need for maintaining the animating spirit of an institution and keeping at bay various inhuman tendencies;

* Growing in creativity and wisdom concerning the establishment of new institutions;

* Gaining the conviction and the character to lead institutions at various levels;

* Developing skills and cultivating gifts that will enable effective leadership and wise care in the shaping of institutions.

What we are here calling institutional leadership could also go under the name of cultural leadership. In the broadest sense, a culture is an intermeshing pattern of institutions, held together by a unifying spiritual vision. Every particular institution also has a culture: its way of handling things, the values around which it is built, the relationships it tends to produce among its members. To be a good leader has much to do with knowing how to build rightly and how to foster a healthy culture in the various institutions within which we live, and to rightly adjust their relationship with each other.

While the form or the culture of an institution or of a society as a whole does not simply determine the lives and behavior of its members, it nonetheless has great importance. It predisposes those under its influence to understand the world and to act in it according to a particular vision. An old architectural saying has it that you first build your house, and then your house builds you. The culture we inhabit will say much about the kind of people we become, individually and together. It should therefore come as no surprise that the call to true leadership, so tied to the leadership of institutions, is by its nature a call to the construction of the overall culture, a call to be attentive to the common good.

True leaders are those who care for the building and maintenance of our human and spiritual community in their proper institutional forms, which is to say, those who build and maintain a genuinely human and Christian culture. This is why true leadership is at its heart a form of charity.

Keeping Institutions Healthy

— NOTES —

AFTERWORD

CHRIST'S CALL TO COURAGEOUS LEADERSHIP

> *Do not be afraid. Do not be satisfied with mediocrity. Put out into the deep and let down your nets for a catch. Let us go forward in hope! A new millennium is opening before the Church like a vast ocean upon which we shall venture, relying on the help of Christ. The Son of God, who became incarnate two thousand years ago out of love for humanity, is at work even today: we need discerning eyes to see this and, above all, a generous heart to become the instruments of his work.*
>
> POPE ST. JOHN PAUL II

IT WAS A watchword of the papacy of John Paul II, a phrase that he repeated on many different occasions: "do not be afraid." We might ask why he returned so often to this theme. Not because he was trying to make people feel vaguely comfortable by mouthing blandly encouraging comments: such a manner of speaking was not his style. It is rather that John Paul recognized fear as one of the besetting temptations of our age, and for good reason. The challenges facing us are many and daunting, enough to put fear into any rational person. Courage is a quality obviously demanded by our time. But the Pope was not simply calling us to look within ourselves and somehow try to manufacture a courageous response. He was instead reminding us of the important and invigorating truth upon which our courage is founded: that we are not alone; that Christ is very much at work in the world.

In the midst of all the challenges and crises and dire possibilities facing humanity, and on a smaller scale facing each person individually, God is not worried. He is not wringing his hands, wondering what he should do or how he can possibly manage things. He is master, and he is using everything a fallen world presents to him to bring about his own will in his own time. There is no reason for Christians to submit to anxiety, whether about the world or about their own lives, as if things were somehow spinning out of control and chaos was looming on the horizon.

It is different for those who have forgotten God's providential care; they will of course be enslaved by all kinds of fears. Those around us who lack the eyes of faith have become highly inventive in creating apocalyptic scenarios, whether environmental or economic or military or societal. Who can blame them? If we humans really are the only ones to "fix" the world, if all depends on our goodness and our strength and our intelligence, then our situation is desperate indeed. But Christians know better than this. Whatever the difficulties we may face, global or personal, we know that they are not outside the care and providence of God. The call to courageous leadership is a call to reality: a summons to see truly what Christ is doing in the world, and to be ready to participate with him as he invites us into that work.

When Ignatius was once speaking with his early disciples, he put a question to them. "If God were to say to you: 'If you want to die at once, I will give you eternal glory; but if you choose to live, I do not guarantee you the gift of final perseverance'; if you thought that by remaining on earth, you would be able to achieve some great thing, what would your choice be?" James Lainez, the man who would eventually succeed Ignatius as general of the order, responded by saying that he would choose the first option, in order to be safe and sure. Ignatius gave an illuminating reply. "For my part," he said, "I wouldn't. If I thought that by continuing to live I could accomplish some great work for God, I would beg Him to leave me on earth till I had done it. I would turn my eyes toward Him and not toward myself. I would take no account of my danger, or my security." Lainez had given a reasonable, even a good answer. But Ignatius was not content with it. He was a man of great soul, and his confident faith spurred him to make a more generous and faith-filled response, trusting in God to carry him through.

Our age once again is looking for those with the spirit of Ignatius. This is a time for magnanimity, for readiness to step forward generously and embrace the leadership Christ teaches and offers. Now is no time for timidity, for carefully consulting our own concerns, for exercising only a feeble faith in the goodness and power of God, for securing a safe place for ourselves and letting others do the great deeds of the day. Why should we be less than we are meant to be in Christ? Why should we settle for leading half a life, when Christ calls us to participate with him in the most important work possible? Christ is on the move: the angels are with him and the saints surround him; he is marching into battle, gathering all who are willing to work with him for the saving of the world. At such a time are we to stand idle, to turn our eyes away, to let him pass us by, to miss our part in the Great Adventure? It may be a hidden work we are called to; it may be one played out before the eyes of the world. Either way, with confidence in God, now is no time to hang back. Life is short, and the world around us is fleeting. With fear behind us, Christ before us, and all good things ahead of us, let us remember the coming everlasting Kingdom, and seize the adventure the Lord is sending us.

TRUE LEADERSHIP

*"This is a vision of integral Christian leadership.
And it takes as its model of leadership, Jesus Christ."*

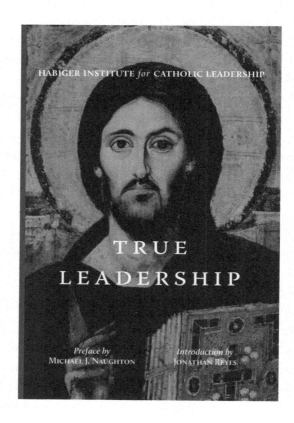

To order, please visit WWW.CLUNYMEDIA.COM.
For bulk orders, please write to INFO@CLUNYMEDIA.COM or
Cluny Media, P.O. Box 1664, Providence, RI 02901.

For information regarding St. Thomas Catholic Studies Habiger Institute,
visit LINK.STTHOMAS.EDU/HABIGER.

Catholic Studies
College of Arts and Sciences

THE HEART OF CULTURE

*"A succinctly substantive history of Western education
and a profound witness to the necessity of maintaining tradition."*

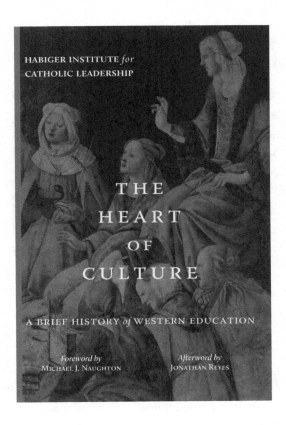

To order, please visit WWW.CLUNYMEDIA.COM.
For bulk orders, please write to INFO@CLUNYMEDIA.COM or
Cluny Media, P.O. Box 1664, Providence, RI 02901.

For information regarding St. Thomas Catholic Studies Habiger Institute,
visit LINK.STTHOMAS.EDU/HABIGER.

Catholic Studies
College of Arts and Sciences

UNIVERSITY OF
St.Thomas

VOCATION *of the* BUSINESS LEADER

A Reflection from the Dicastery
for Promoting Integral Human Development

Originally published in 2012 (and now available in 16 languages) as a
handbook and guide for business professionals and educators,
Vocation of the Business Leader is a valuable resource for articulating
the ethical and spiritual meaning of the vocation of the leader and of
organizations today. Print copies of the document are now available
to order for $6.00 U.S. per copy (plus shipping) with discounts over 100.

To order *Vocation of the Business Leader,* or to see articles, curriculum
and translations of the document, please visit STTHOMAS.EDU/RYANINSTITUTE.

Catholic Studies
College of Arts and Sciences
UNIVERSITY OF
St.Thomas

BE
transformed

Earn your MA in Catholic Studies
from the largest and oldest program in the field.

link.stthomas.edu/CSMA

Scholarships available

Catholic Studies
College of Arts and Sciences

UNIVERSITY OF
St.Thomas

CLUNY MEDIA

Designed by Fiona Cecile Clarke, the CLUNY MEDIA *logo
depicts a monk at work in the scriptorium,
with a cat sitting at his feet.*

*The monk represents our mission to emulate
the invaluable contributions of the monks
of Cluny in preserving the libraries of the West,
our strivings to know and love the truth.*

*The cat at the monk's feet is Pangur Bán, from the
eponymous Irish poem of the 9th century.
The anonymous poet compares his scholarly
pursuit of truth with the cat's happy hunting of mice.
The depiction of Pangur Bán is an homage to the work
of the monks of Irish monasteries and a sign
of the joy we at Cluny take in our trade.*

"Messe ocus Pangur Bán,
cechtar nathar fria saindan:
bíth a menmasam fri seilgg,
mu memna céin im saincheirdd."